Armenian Literature

Various Contributors
Edited by: Alfred Aghajanian

Armenian Literature

Copyright © 2012 by Indo-European Publishing

Contact:
IndoEuropeanPublishing@gmail.com

The present edition is a reproduction of 1901 publication of this work, produced in the current edition with completely new, easy to read format by Indo-European Publishing.

For an authentic reading experience, the Spelling, punctuation, and capitalization have been retained from the original text.

ISBN: 978-1-60444-738-5

IndoEuropean
Publishing.com
Los Angeles, CA, USA

EDITOR'S PREFACE

Being of Armenian decent, and having gone through Mekhitarian Armenological Studies, I was naturally drawn to this rich volume on the subject of Armenian literature. I find the special introduction by Robert Arnot informative and intriguing. He has adequately depicted the state and the nature of the Armenian literature up until the late nineteenth and early twentieth centuries, especially as it pertains to the Armenian ecclesiastical establishment of the period.

Despite the evidence that much of the Armenian Pagan literature was lost when Armenia became the first nation to accept Christianity as its state religion, on 301 C.E. (A.D.), the Armenian Church fostered a rich literature and a vast amount of literary works, albeit different than that of the pagan literature. The most worthy example of fostering this new Armenian literature is the first translation of the bible from its original text in the fifth century. This work, along with other translations of original works, such as the rendering of Aristotle and of the romance of Alexander, is still closely studied today by scholars who seek to examine the closest translated texts to the original works. Aside from ecclesiastical works, there has also been much traditional and nationalistic epic poetry, the best-known of which is probably the David of Sassoun (Sasountsi David - Սասունցի Դավիթ, as the Armenians call it), which is included in this volume.

Throughout the centuries, Armenian literature has gone through several major revival periods. The Armenian literary works were mostly stagnant in the Armenian territory in the sixteenth century when Armenia was invaded by the Persians. The result was that the literate Armenians were scattered to throughout Europe and beyond. In a sense, the Persian invasion was going to be a positive force in revival of the Armenian literature. The scattered Armenians in

Diaspora established printing shops in various European cities, such as Venice, Rome, Limburg, Milan, Paris, and many other European and later Asian cities. Old literatures were republished and new ones were created in abundance. The Mekhitarists of Venice, a community of Catholic Armenian monks, have been the frontrunner in this revival. Other centers responsible for the major revival of Armenian literature in fifteenth through nineteenth centuries were Russia, Constantinople, and Etchmiadzin in proper Armenia (The first in the world church style building was re-built on the top of
a pagan temple in 484 C.E. in Etchmiadzin and today it is the seat of the Catholicos of all Armenians).
The sixteenth century brought about an intriguing way of further propagating the Armenian literature; the beloved Armenian troubadours' tradition. Divided between the Ottoman Empire and Safavid Persia, the Armenians developed the troubadour tradition. A troubadour, called ashough (աշուղ) in Armenian, would go from town to town, and would often recite his literature to the ordinary people. The most successful ashough at the time was Sayat Nova whose talent was so impressive that he performed in the courts of Kings and Meliks. Sayat Nova often recounted about his feelings for his beloved mistress by using the popular language rather than the Classical Armenian, which was obsolete and foreign outside churches and schools.

The mainstream Armenian literature did not embrace the popular language (now modern Armenian) until Khachatur Abovian (1804-1848) created the now modern Armenian literature. Abovian abandoned the classical Armenian language and used the modern (everyday speaking) language for his works of grandeur. This was a revolutionary undertaking that would change the nature of Armenian literature forever. It would bring the Armenian literature closer to the Armenian masses, and by doing so, create an
unparallel resurgence of Armenian literature. Abovian was the main player of the literary movement in the nineteenth century that was responsible for the period of time during which Armenian literature flourished. This period of time is

of utmost significance for Armenian literature and is known as the Revival Period (Zartonk - Զարթոնք in Armenian).

The literary tradition of Khachatur Abovian, and his followers such as Mikael Nalbandian and Raffi was continued even as Armenia came under communist rule. This revival of tradition continued in the Soviet era thanks to such writers and poets as Hovhannes Tumanyan, Yeghishe Charents and others. In the late 1960's a new generation of Armenian writers emerged. As Armenian history of the 1920's and of the 1915 Armenian Genocide came to be more openly discussed, writers like Paruyr Sevak, Gevork Emin, Silva Kaputikyan and Hovhannes Shiraz began a new era of literature. Since the independence of Armenia in 1991, despite the post Soviet Union difficulties and economic struggles , a new breed of Armenian writers emerged, both from inside Armenia and from the Diaspora making sure that Armenian Literature holds its significance and grandeur in global literature.

Robert Arnot was an expert on Armenian literature and has written a great introduction to this volume; it would have been interesting to know his thoughts about the recent modern Armenian literature as well. Alas, he is not with us to enlighten us of that regard. Nevertheless his contribution to this volume on Armenian literature is much appreciated for his clever analysis is his special introduction and masterful translation of the Armenian poems.

Alfred Aghajanian

CONTENTS

SPECIAL INTRODUCTION

The literature of ancient Armenia that is still extant is meager in quantity and to a large extent ecclesiastical in tone. To realize its oriental color one must resort entirely to that portion which deals with the home life of the people, with their fasts and festivals, their emotions, manners, and traditions. The ecclesiastical character of much of the early Armenian literature is accounted for by the fact that Christianity was preached there in the first century after Christ, by the apostles Thaddeus and Bartholomew, and that the Armenian Church is the oldest national Christian Church in the world.

It is no doubt owing to the conversion of the entire Armenian nation under the passionate preaching of Gregory the Illuminator that most of the literary products, of primitive Armenia—the mythological legends and chants of heroic deeds sung by bards—are lost. The Church would have none of them. Gregory not only destroyed the pagan temples, but he sought to stamp out the pagan literature— the poetry and recorded traditions that celebrated the deeds of gods and goddesses and of national heroes. He would have succeeded, too, had not the romantic spirit of the race clung fondly to their ballads and folk-lore. Ecclesiastical historiographers in referring to those times say quaintly enough, meaning to censure the people, that in spite of their great religious advantages the Armenians persisted in singing some of their heathen ballads as late as the twelfth century. Curiously enough, we owe the fragments we possess of early Armenian poetry to these same ecclesiastical critics. These fragments suggest a popular poesy, stirring and full of powerful imagery, employed mostly in celebrating royal marriages, religious feasts, and containing dirges for the dead, and ballads of customs—not a wide field, but one invaluable to the philologist and to ethnological students.
The Christian chroniclers and critics, however, while preserving but little of the verse of early Armenia, have

1

handed down to us many legends and traditions, though they relate them, unfortunately, with much carelessness and with a contempt for detail that is often exasperating to one seeking for instructive parallelisms between the heroic legends of different nations. Evidently the only object of the ecclesiastical chroniclers in preserving these legends was to invest their descriptions of the times with a local color. Even Moses of Chorene [Movses Khorenatzi], who by royal command collected many of these legends, and in his sympathetic treatment of them evinces poetic genius and keen literary appreciation, fails to realize the importance of his task. After speaking of the old Armenian kings with enthusiasm, and even condoning their paganism for the sake of their virility, he leaves his collection in the utmost disorder and positively without a note or comment. In the face of such difficulties, therefore, it has been hard to present specimens of early Armenian folk-lore and legends that shall give the reader a rightful idea of the race and the time.

As Armenia was the highroad between Asia and Europe, these old stories and folk-plays show the influence of migrating and invading people. The mythology of the Chaldeans and Persians mingles oddly with traditions purely Armenian. This is well shown in the story of David of Sassun, given in this volume. David was the local hero of the place where Moses of Chorene [Movses Khorenatzi] was born and probably spent his declining years, after years of literary labor and study in Athens and Alexandria. The name of the district was Mush, and close by the monastery in which Moses was buried lies the village of Sassun.

David's history is rich in personal incident, and recalls to the reader the tales related of the Persian Izdubar, the Chaldeo-Babylonian Nimrod, and the Greek Heracles. He is as much the hero of the tale as is Joseph Andrews in Fielding's classic of that name. His marvelous strength is used as handily for a jest as for some prodigious victory over man or monster. He is drawn for us as a bold, reckless fellow, with a rollicking sense of humor, which, in truth, sits but awkwardly upon the intense devotion to the Cross and its demands with which

2

Moses or some later redactor has seen fit to burden this purely pagan hero. David is very human in spite of his blood-stained club and combative instincts, and his kindliness and bonhomie awake in us a passing disappointment at his untimely demise.

If we except some ecclesiastical writings, these fragments preserved by Movses of Khoren [Movses Khorenatzi] and others comprehend all that is left to us of the literature of Armenia antedating the Persian invasion. After the Persian flood of fire and sword had rolled over this Asiatic Poland, the stricken Christian Church revived. A monk named Mesrop set to work to revive the spirit of literature. His difficulties were great. It was not alone the resuscitating of a dead literary desire, but it entailed also the providing of a vehicle of expression, namely an alphabet, so deeply had the Persian domination imprinted itself upon the land. As might be expected, the primary results of the revival were didactic, speculative, or religious in character. Mysticism at that time flourished in the monasteries, and the national spirit—the customs, habits, joys, and emotions of the people—had not yet found re-expression in script. The Church became the dominant power in literature, and if it is true on the one hand that the Armenian people lost intellectual independence, it is also true on the other that they gained that religious zeal and strength which enabled them as an entity—a united race—to survive the fatal day of Avarair [Battle of Avarayr], where, under the shadow of hoary Ararat, the Armenian Marathon was fought and lost, and Vartan, their national hero, died. All sorts of traditions cluster still around the battlefield of Avarair [Avarayr]. A species of red flower grows there that is nowhere else to be found, and it is commonly believed that this red blossom sprang originally from the blood of the slain Armenian warriors. On the plain of Avarair [Avarayr] is also found a small antelope with a pouch upon its breast secreting musk—a peculiarity gained, they say, from feeding on grass soaked with the blood of Armenia's sons. And at Avarair [Avarayr], too, it is said that the lament of the nightingales is ever, "Vartan, Vartan." The story of these times is preserved in fragments in the religious chronicles of Lazarus of Pharb

3

and of Eliseus. When, during the Persian domination, Armenia became entirely shut off from the avenues of Greek culture, and was left unaided in her struggle for national existence, the light of literature again sank to a feeble gleam. There was, indeed, a faint revival in the tenth century, and again a second and a stronger renaissance in the twelfth under the impulse given by Nerses, and by his namesake, the Patriarch. But this revival, like the former, was not general in character. It was mostly a revival of religious mysticism in literature, not of the national spirit, though to this epoch belong the choicest hymnological productions of the Armenian Church.

There are no chronicles extant that can be called purely Armenian. The oldest chronicles that we have of Armenia—and there are many—wander off into the histories of other people—of the Byzantines, for instance, and even of the Crusaders. The passages that deal with Armenia are devoted almost entirely to narrating the sufferings of the Armenians under the successive invasions of pagans and Mahometans, and the efforts made to keep the early Christian faith—forming almost a national book of martyrs, and setting forth a tragic romance of perpetual struggle. These records cannot be called Armenian literature in a real sense, for in many cases they were not written by Armenians, but they picture in vivid fashion the trials suffered by Armenians at the hands of invading nations, and the sacrifices made to preserve a national existence. They picture, in pages bristling with horrible detail, the sacrifices and sufferings of a desperate people, and in them we see Armenia as the prophet saw Judea, "naked, lying by the wayside, trodden under foot by all nations." These chronicles have an interest all their own, but they lack literary beauty, and not being, in themselves, Armenian literature, have not been included in the selections made as being purely representative of the race and land.

The examples of Armenian proverbs and folk-lore included in this volume show, as is usual, the ethnological relationship that is so easily traced between the fables of Aesop, of Bidpai, of Vartan, and of Loqman. It may be said

4

with truth that in the folk-lore and fables of all nations can be traced kinship of imagination, with a variety of application that differs with the customs and climate of the people. But the Armenian is especially rich in a variety of elements. We meet enchantments, faculties, superstitions, and abstract ideas personified, which are supposed to attach miraculous meanings to the most ordinary events. Dreams, riddles, and the like—all are there. The one strange personification is the Dew. The Dew is a monster, half demon, half human; sometimes harmless, sometimes malevolent; mortal, indeed, but reaching a good or, shall we say, an evil old age. The Dew figures in nearly all Armenian fairy-tales.

The Armenian proverbs exhibit the persistent capacity of the Armenians during a time of *Sturm und Drang* to embody, in pithy, wise, and sometimes cynical form, the wisdom drawn from their own experience and from that of the ages. It is possible that the cynical vein discernible in some of these proverbs is a result of the intense and continued national trials. Take, for instance, this proverb, "If a brother were a good thing, God would have provided himself with one." Can anything be more cynical?

The poems are of later origin. Since the twelfth century, when literature burst the bonds imposed upon it by ecclesiastical domination, the poetic spirit of the Armenians has found expression. It is rich in oriental passion and imagery, brilliant in expression, and intensely musical. But through all the poems we are reminded of the melancholy strain that pervaded the exiles of Jerusalem when "by the waters of Babylon" they "sat down and wept." The apostrophe to Araxes reminds us of the trials of Armenia, of her exiled sons, of her wasted land, and of the perpetual fast she ever keeps in mourning for her children.

The comedy of "The Ruined Family" and the pathetic story of "The Vacant Yard" are also of the post-monastic era. In the comedy we gain an insight into the jealousy and the pride of life that pervaded then as now the middle walks of life. Its Ibsenesque [dramatic] quality is very striking. The

5

persistent and human struggle of the mother to gain a high position in life for her daughter through marriage, and the agonizing of the father to get together a suitable dower for his daughter, together with the worldly-wise comments and advice of the old aunt, are so true to modern life that one realizes anew the sameness of human nature in all climes and ages.

"The Vacant Yard" gives us a charming picture of Armenian life. The people are depicted with an impartial pen, subject to the minor crosses and humors of fate, having their ups and downs just as we do to-day, but the intense local color that pervades the story holds one to the closing line.

As a people the Armenians cannot boast of as vast a literature as the Persians, their one-time conquerors, but that which remains of purely Armenian prose, folk-lore, and poetry tells us of a poetic race, gifted with imaginative fire, sternness of will, and persistency of adherence to old ideas, a race that in proportion to their limited production in letters can challenge comparison with any people.

Robert Arnot

PROVERBS AND FOLK-LORE
[*Translated by F.B. Collins, B.S.*]

≈ I know many songs, but I cannot sing.

≈ When a man sees that the water does not follow him, he follows the water.

≈ When a tree falls there is plenty of kindling wood.

≈ He who falls into the water need have no fear of rain.

≈ A good swimmer finds death in the water.

≈ Strong vinegar bursts the cask.

≈ Dogs quarrel among themselves, but against the wolf they are united.

≈ God understands the dumb.

≈ Only he who can read is a man.

≈ The chick shows itself in the egg, the child in the cradle.

≈ What a man acquires in his youth serves as a crutch in his old age.

≈ One wit is good; two wits are better.

≈ Begin with small things, that you may achieve great.

≈ A devil with experience is better than an angel without.

≈ What the great say, the humble hear.

≈ He who steals an egg will steal a horse also.

7

≈ Turn the spit, so that neither meat nor roasting-iron shall burn.

≈ One can spoil the good name of a thousand.

≈ What manner of things thou speakest of, such shalt thou also hear.

≈ The grandfather ate unripe grapes, and the grandson's teeth were set on edge.

≈ One bad deed begets another.

≈ Go home when the table is set, and to church when it is almost over.

≈ A devil at home, a parson abroad.

≈ God created men and women: who, then, created monks? Poor and proud.

≈ In dreams the hungry see bread and the thirsty water.

≈ Ere the fat become lean, the lean are already dead.

≈ Wish for a cow for your neighbor, that God may give you two.

≈ What is play to the cat is death to the mouse.

≈ Unless the child cries, the mother will not suckle it.

≈ A fish in the water is worth nothing.

≈ Gold is small but of great worth.

≈ At home the dog is very brave.

≈ Observe the mother ere you take the daughter.

≈ If you lose half and then leave off, something is gained.

≈ The good mourn for what was taken away, the wolf for what was left behind.

≈ Only a bearded man can laugh at a beardless face.

≈ He descends from a horse and seats himself on an ass.

≈ No other day can equal the one that is past.

≈ When a man grows rich, he thinks his walls are awry.

≈ Make friends with a dog, but keep a stick in your hand.

≈ One should not feel hurt at the kick of an ass.

≈ The blind have no higher wish than to have two eyes.

≈ The thief wants only a dark night.

≈ A thief robbed another thief, and God marveled at it in heaven.

≈ He who has money has no sense; and he who has sense, no money.

≈ He who begs is shameless, but still more shameless is he who lends not to him.

≈ Better lose one's eyes than one's calling.

≈ What the wind brings it will take away again.

≈ A bad dog neither eats himself nor gives to others.

≈ Running is also an art.

≈ Only in the bath can one tell black from white.

≈ Water is sure to find its way.

≈ What does the blind care if candles are dear?

≈ Speak little and you will hear much.

≈ No one is sure that his light will burn till morning.

≈ He who speaks the truth must have one foot in the stirrup.

≈ The more you stone a dog the more he barks.

≈ One blossom does not make a spring.

≈ One hand cannot clap alone.

≈ Strike the iron while it is hot.

≈ Take up a stick, and the thieving dog understands.

≈ Corruption illumines dark paths.

≈ When they laid down the law to the wolf, he said, "Be quiet, or the sheep will run away."

≈ One hears Ali is dead; but one knows not which one.

≈ The scornful soon grow old.

≈ Who shall work? I and thou. Who shall eat? I and thou.

≈ Stay in the place where there is bread.

≈ If bread tastes good, it is all one to me whether a Jew or a Turk bakes it.

≈ One loves the rose, another the lilac.

≈ Before Susan had done prinking, church was over.

≈ The simpleton went to the wedding and said, "Indeed, it is much better here than it is at home."

≈ He sleeps for himself and dreams for others.

≈ The flower falls under the bush.

≈ Not everything round is an apple.

≈ What does an ass know about almonds?

≈ A king must be worthy of a crown.

≈ When you are going in consider first how you are coming out.

≈ What thou canst do to-day leave not until to-morrow.

≈ The rose of winter-time is fire.

≈ The end of strife is repentance.

≈ From the same flower the serpent draws poison and the bees honey.

≈ My heart is no table-cover to be spread over everything.

≈ As long as the wagon is not upset the way is not mended.

≈ The water that drowns me is for me an ocean.

≈ The Armenian has his understanding in his head, the Georgian in his eyes.

≈ The ass knows seven ways of swimming, but when he sees the water he forgets them all.

≈ The wound of a dagger heals, but that of the tongue, never.

≈ A good ox is known in the yoke, a good woman at the cradle of her child.

≈ Love ever so well, there is also hate; hate ever so much, there is always love.

≈ A shrewd enemy is better than a stupid friend.

≈ To rise early is not everything; happy are they who have the help of God.

≈ A dress that is not worn wears itself out.

≈ I came from the ocean and was drowned in a spoonful of water.

≈ Because the cat could get no meat, he said, "To-day is Friday."

≈ The house that a woman builds God will not destroy; but a woman is likely to destroy the house that God has built.

≈ The dowry a woman brings into the house is a bell.

≈ Whenever you come near, the clapper strikes in your face.

≈ By asking, one finds the way to Jerusalem.

≈ Which of the five fingers can you cut off without hurting yourself?

≈ The father's kingdom is the son's mite.

≈ Far from the eye, far from the heart.

≈ If a brother was really good for anything, God would have one.

≈ When God gives, He gives with both hands.

≈ A daughter is a treasure which belongs to another.

≈ The world is a pair of stairs: some go up and others go down.

≈ The poor understand the troubles of the poor.

≈ The childless have one trouble, but those who have children have a thousand.

≈ God turns away his face from a shameless man.

≈ The eyes would not disagree even if the nose were not between them.

≈ Until you see trouble you will never know joy.

≈ You never know a man until you have eaten a barrel of salt with him.

≈ Every man's own trouble is as large as a camel.

≈ The goat prefers one goat to a whole herd of sheep.

≈ The fox has destroyed the world, and the wolf has lost his calling.

≈ The fool throws himself into the stream, and forty wise men cannot pull him out.

≈ A near neighbor is better than a distant kinsman.

≈ When I have honey, the flies come even from Bagdad.

≈ A guest comes from God.

≈ The guest is the ass of the inn-keeper.

≈ When everything is cheap the customer has no conscience.

THE SHEEP-BROTHER

Once there was a widow and she had a daughter. The widow married a widower who had by his first wife two children, a boy and a girl. The wife was always coaxing her husband: "Take the children, do, and lead them up into the mountains." Her husband could not refuse her, and, lo! One day he put some bread in his basket, took the children, and set off for the mountain.

They went on and on and came to a strange place. Then the father said to the children, "Rest here a little while," and the children sat down to rest. The father turned his face away and wept bitterly, very bitterly. Then he turned again to the children and said, "Eat something," and they ate. Then the boy said, "Father, dear, I want a drink." The father took his staff, stuck it into the ground, threw his coat over it, and said, "Come here, my son, sit in the shadow of my coat, and I will get you some water." The brother and sister stayed and the father went away and forsook his children. Whether they waited a long time or a short time before they saw that their father was not coming back is not known. They wandered here and there looking for him, but saw no human being anywhere.

At last they came back to the same spot, and, beginning to weep, they said:

"Alas! Alas! See, here is father's staff, and here is his coat, and he comes not, and he comes not."

Whether the brother and sister sat there a long time or a short time is not known. They rose after a while, and one took the staff and the other the coat, and they went away without knowing whither. They went on and on and on, until they saw tracks of horses' hoofs filled with rain-water.

"I am going to drink, sister," said the brother.

"Do not drink, little brother, or you will become a colt," said the sister.

They passed on till they saw tracks of oxen's hoofs.

"O sister dear, how thirsty I am!"

"Do not drink, little brother, or you will be a calf," the sister said to him.

14

They went on till they saw the tracks of buffalo hoofs.

"O sister dear, how thirsty I am!"

"Drink not, little brother, or you will be a buffalo calf."

They passed on and saw the tracks of bears' paws.

"Oh, I am so thirsty, sister dear."

"Drink not, little brother, or you will become a little bear."

They went on and saw the tracks of swine's trotters.

"O sister dear, I am going to drink."

"Drink not, little brother, or you will become a little pig."

They went on and on till they saw the tracks of the pads of wolves.

"O sister dear, how thirsty I am!"

"Do not drink, little brother, or you will become a little wolf."

They walked on and on till they saw the tracks of sheep's trotters.

"O sister dear, I am almost dying with thirst."

"O little brother, you grieve me so! You will, indeed, be a sheep if you drink."

He could stand it no longer. He drank and turned into a sheep. He began to bleat and ran after his sister. Long they wandered, and at last came home.

Then the stepmother began to scheme against them. She edged up to her husband and said: "Kill your sheep. I want to eat him."

The sister got her sheep-brother away in the nick of time and drove him back into the mountains. Every day she drove him to the meadows and she spun linen. Once her distaff fell from her hand and rolled into a cavern. The sheep-brother stayed behind grazing while she went to get the distaff.

She stepped into the cavern and saw lying in a corner a Dew, one thousand years old. She suddenly spied the girl and said: "Neither the feathered birds nor the crawling serpent can make their way in here; how then hast thou, maiden, dared to enter?"

The girl spoke up in her fright. "For love of you I came here, dear grandmother."

The old Dew mother bade the girl come near and

15

asked her this and that. The maiden pleased her very much. "I will go and bring you a fish," she said, "you are certainly hungry." But the fishes were snakes and dragons. The girl was sorely frightened and began to cry with terror. The old Dew said, "Maiden, why do you weep?" She answered, "I have just thought of my mother, and for her sake I weep." Then she told the old mother everything that had happened to her. "If that is so," said the Dew, "sit down here and I will lay my head on your knee and go to sleep."

She made up the fire, stuck the poker into the stove, and said:

"When the devil flies by do not waken me. If the rainbow-colored one passes near, take the glowing poker from the stove and lay it on my foot."

The maiden's heart crept into her heels from fright. What was she to do? She sat down, the Dew laid her head on her knees and slept. Soon she saw a horrible black monster flying by. The maiden was silent. After a while there came flying by a rainbow-colored creature. She seized the glowing poker and threw it on the old Dew's foot. The old mother awoke and said, "Phew, how the fleas bite." She rose and lifted up the maiden. The girl's hair and clothing were turned to gold from the splendor of the rainbow colors. She kissed the old Dew's hand and begged that she might go. She went away, and taking her sheep-brother with her started for home. The stepmother was not there, and the maiden secretly dug a hole, buried her golden dress, and sat down and put on an old one.

The stepmother came home and saw that the maiden had golden hair.

"What have you done to your hair to make it like gold?" she asked. The maiden told her all, how and when. The next day the stepmother sent her own daughter to the same mountain. The stepmother's daughter purposely let her distaff fall and it rolled into the hole. She went in to get it, but the old Dew mother turned her into a scarecrow and sent her home.

About that time there was a wedding in the royal castle; the King was giving one of his sons in marriage, and the people came from all directions to look on and enjoy themselves.

The stepmother threw on a kerchief and smartened up the head of her daughter and took her to see the wedding. The girl with the golden hair did not stay at home, but, putting on her golden dress so that she became from head to foot a gleaming houri, she went after them.

But on the way home, she ran so fast to get there before her stepmother, that she dropped one of her golden shoes in the fountain. When they led the horses of the King's second son to drink, the horses caught sight of the golden shoe in the water and drew back and would not drink. The King caused the wise men to be called, and asked them to make known the reason why the horses would not drink, and they found only the golden shoe. The King sent out his herald to tell the people that he would marry his son to whomsoever this shoe fitted.

He sent people throughout the whole city to try on the shoe, and they came to the house where the sheep-brother was. The stepmother pushed the maiden with the golden locks into the stove, and hid her, and showed only her own daughter.

A cock came up to the threshold and crowed three times, "Cock-a-doodle doo! The fairest of the fair is in the stove." The King's people brushed the stepmother aside and led the maiden with golden hair from the stove, tried on the shoe, which fitted as though moulded to the foot.

"Now stand up," said they, "and you shall be a royal bride."

The maiden put on her golden dress, drove her sheep-brother before her, and went to the castle. She was married to the King's son, and seven days and seven nights they feasted.

Again the stepmother took her daughter and went to the castle to visit her stepdaughter, who in spite of all treated her as her mother and invited her into the castle garden. From the garden they went to the seashore and sat down to rest. The stepmother said, "Let us bathe in the sea." While they were bathing she pushed the wife of the King's son far out into the water, and a great fish came swimming by and swallowed her.

Meanwhile the stepmother put the golden dress on her own daughter and led her to the royal castle and placed her in the seat where the young wife always sat, covering her face and her head so that no one would know her.

The young wife sat in the fish and heard the voice of the bell-ringer. She called to him and pleaded: "Bell-ringer, O bell-ringer, thou hast called the people to church; cross thyself seven times, and I entreat thee, in the name of heaven, go to the prince and say that they must not slaughter my sheep-brother."

Once, twice the bell-ringer heard this voice and told the King's son about it.

The King's son took the bell-ringer with him and went at night to the seashore. The same voice spoke the same words. He knew that it was his dear wife that spoke, and drew his sword and ripped open the fish and helped his loved one out.

They went home, and the prince had the stepmother brought to him, and said to her: "Mother-in-law, tell me what kind of a present you would like: a horse fed with barley or a knife with a black handle?"

The stepmother answered: "Let the knife with a black handle pierce the breast of thine enemy; but give me the horse fed with barley."

The King's son commanded them to tie the stepmother and her daughter to the tail of a horse, and to hunt them over mountain and rock till nothing was left of them but their ears and a tuft of hair.

After that the King's son lived happily with his wife and her sheep-brother. The others were punished and she rejoiced.

And three apples fell down from heaven.

THE YOUTH WHO WOULD NOT
TELL HIS DREAM

There lived once upon a time a man and wife who had a son. The son arose from his sleep one morning and said to his mother: "Mother dear, I had a dream, but what it was I will not tell you."

The mother said, "Why will you not tell me?"

"I will not, and that settles it," answered the youth, and his mother seized him and cudgeled him well.

Then he went to his father and said to him: "Father dear, I had a dream, but what it was I would not tell mother, nor will I tell you," and his father also gave him a good flogging. He began to sulk and ran away from home. He walked and walked the whole day long and, meeting a traveler, said after greeting him: "I had a dream, but what it was I would tell neither father nor mother and I will not tell you," Then he went on his way till finally he came to the Emir's house and said to the Emir: "Emir, I had a dream, but what it was I would tell neither father nor mother, nor yet the traveler, and I will not tell you."

The Emir had him seized and thrown into the garret, where he began to cut through the floor with a knife he managed to get from some one of the Emir's people. He cut and cut until he made an opening over the chamber of the Emir's daughter, who had just filled a plate with food and gone away. The youth jumped down, emptied the plate, ate what he wanted, and crept back into the garret. The second, third, and fourth days he did this also, and the Emir's daughter could not think who had taken away her meal. The next day she hid herself under the table to watch and find out. Seeing the youth jump down and begin to eat from her plate, she rushed out and said to him, "Who are you?"

"I had a dream, but what it was I would tell neither father nor mother, nor the traveler, nor yet the Emir. The Emir shut me up in the garret. Now everything depends on you; do with me what you will."

19

The youth looked at the maiden, and they loved each other and saw each other every day.

The King of the West came to the King of the East to court the daughter of the King of the East for his son. He sent an iron bar with both ends shaped alike and asked: "Which is the top and which is the bottom? If you can guess that, good! If not, I will carry your daughter away with me."

The King asked everybody, but nobody could tell. The King's daughter told her lover about it and he said: "Go tell your father the Emir to throw the bar into a brook. The heavy end will sink. Make a hole in that end and send the bar back to the King of the West." And it happened that he was right, and the messengers returned to their King.

The King of the West sent three horses of the same size and color and asked: "Which is the one-year-old, which is the two-year-old, and which the mare? If you can guess that, good. If not, then I will carry off your daughter."

The King of the East collected all the clever people, but no one could guess. He was helpless and knew not what to do. Then his daughter went to her lover and said, "They are going to take me away," and she told him when and how.

The youth said: "Go and say to your father, 'Dip a bundle of hay in water, strew it with salt, and put it near the horses' stall. In the morning the mare will come first, the two-year-old second, the one-year-old last.'"

They did this and sent the King of the West his answer.

He waited a little and sent a steel spear and a steel shield, and said: "If you pierce the shield with the spear, I will give my daughter to your son. If not, send your daughter to my son."

Many people tried, and among them the King himself, but they could find no way of piercing the shield. The King's daughter told him of her beloved prisoner, and the King sent for him. The youth thrust the spear into the ground, and, striking the shield against it, pierced it through.

As the King had no son, he sent the youth in place of a son to the King of the West to demand his daughter, according to agreement.

He went on and on—how long it is not known—and saw someone with his ear to the ground listening.

"Who are you?" the youth asked.

"I am he who hears everything that is said in the whole world."

"This is a brave fellow," said the youth. "He knows everything that is said in the world."

"I am no brave fellow. He who has pierced a steel shield with a steel spear is a brave fellow," was the answer.

"I am he," said the youth. "Let us be brothers."

They journeyed on together and saw a man with a millstone on each foot, and one leg stepped toward Chisan and the other toward Stambul [Istanbul].

"That seems to me a brave fellow! One leg steps toward Chisan and the other toward Stambul [Istanbul]."

"I am no brave fellow. He who has pierced a steel shield with a steel spear is a brave fellow," said the man with the millstones.

"I am he. Let us be brothers."

They were three and they journeyed on together.

They went on and on and saw a mill with seven millstones grinding corn. And one man ate all and was not satisfied, but grumbled and said, "O little father, I die of hunger."

"That is a brave fellow," said the youth. "Seven millstones grind for him and yet he has not enough, but cries, 'I die of hunger.'"

"I am no brave fellow. He who pierced a steel shield with a steel spear is a brave fellow," said the hungry man.

"I am he. Let us be brothers," said the youth and the four journeyed on together. They went on and on and saw a man who had loaded the whole world on his back and even wished to lift it up.

"That is a brave fellow. He has loaded himself with the whole world and wishes to lift it up," said the youth.

"I am no brave fellow. He who has pierced a steel shield with a steel spear is a brave fellow," said the burdened man.

"I am he. Let us be brothers."

The five journeyed on together. They went on and on and saw a man lying in a brook and he sipped up all its waters and yet cried, "O little father, I am parched with thirst."

21

"That is a brave fellow. He drinks up the whole brook and still says he is thirsty," said the youth.

"I am no brave fellow. He who has pierced a steel shield with a steel spear is a brave fellow," said the thirsty man.

"I am he. Let us be brothers."

The six journeyed on together. They went on and on and saw a shepherd who was playing the pipes, and mountains and valleys, fields and forests, men and animals, danced to the music.

"That seems to me to be a brave fellow. He makes mountains and valleys dance," said the youth.

"I am no brave fellow. He who has pierced a steel shield with a steel spear is a brave fellow," said the musical man.

"I am he. Let us be brothers," said the youth.

The seven journeyed on together.

"Brother who hast pierced a steel shield with a steel spear, whither is God leading us?"

"We are going to get the daughter of the King of the West," said the youth.

"Only you can marry her," said they all.

They went on till they came to the King's castle, but when they asked for the daughter the King would not let her go, but called his people together and said: "They have come after the bride. They are not very hungry, perhaps they will eat only a bite or two. Let one-and-twenty ovens be filled with bread and make one-and-twenty kettles of soup. If they eat all this I will give them my daughter; otherwise, I will not."

The seven brothers were in a distant room. He who listened with his ear to the ground heard what the King commanded, and said:

"Brother who hast pierced a steel shield with a steel spear, do you understand what the King said?"

"Rascal! how can I know what he says when I am not in the same room with him? What did he say?"

"He has commanded them to bake bread in one-and-twenty ovens and to make one-and-twenty kettles of soup. If we eat it all, we can take his daughter; otherwise, not."

The brother who devoured all the meal that seven

22

millstones, ground said: "Fear not, I will eat everything that comes to hand, and then cry, 'Little father, I die of hunger.'"

When the King saw the hungry man eat he screamed: "May he perish! I shall certainly meet defeat at his hands."

Again he called his people to him and said, "Kindle a great fire, strew it with ashes and cover it with blankets. When they come in in the evening they will be consumed, all seven of them."

The brother with the sharp ears said: "Brother who hast pierced a steel shield with a steel spear, do you understand what the King said?"

"No; how can I know what he said?"

"He said, 'Kindle a fire, strew it with ashes, and cover it with blankets, and when they come in in the evening they will be consumed, all seven of them.'"

Then said the brother who drank up the brook: "I will drink all I can and go in before you. I will spit it all out and turn the whole house into a sea."

In the evening they begged the King to allow them to rest in the room set apart for them. The water-drinker filled the whole room with water, and they went into another.

The King lost his wits and knew not what to do. He called his people together, and they said in one voice, "Let what will happen, we will not let our princess go!"

The man with the sharp ears heard them, and said, "Brother who hast pierced a steel shield with a steel spear, do you understand what the King said?"

"How should I know what he said?"

"He said, 'Let what will happen, I will not let my daughter go.'"

The brother who had loaded himself with the whole world said: "Wait, I will take his castle and all his land on my back and carry it away."

He took the castle on his back and started off. The shepherd played on his pipes, and mountains and valleys danced to the music. He who had fastened millstones to his feet led the march, and they all went joyously forward, making a great noise.

The King began to weep, and begged them to leave him his castle. "Take my daughter with you. You have earned her."

They put the castle back in its place, the shepherd stopped playing, and mountain and valley stood still. They took the King's daughter and departed, and each hero returned to his dwelling-place, and he who had pierced the steel shield with the steel spear took the maiden and came again to the King of the East. And the King of the East gave him his own daughter, whom the youth had long loved, for his wife. So he had two wives—one was the daughter of the King of the East, the other the daughter of the King of the West.

At night, when they lay down to sleep, he said: "Now, I have one sun on one side and another sun on the other side, and a bright star plays on my breast."

In the morning he sent for his parents and called also the King to him, and said, "Now, I will tell my dream." "What was it, then?" they all said. He answered: "I saw in my dream one sun on one side of me and another sun on the other, and a bright star played on my breast."

"Had you such a dream?" they asked.

"I swear I had such a dream."

And three apples fell from heaven: one for the story-teller, one for him who made him tell it, and one for the hearer.

THE VACANT YARD
[Translated by E.B. Collins, B.S.]

Several days ago I wished to visit an acquaintance, but it chanced he was not at home. I came therefore through the gate again out into the street, and stood looking to right and left and considering where I could go. In front of me lay a vacant yard, which was, I thought, not wholly like other vacant yards. On it was neither house nor barn nor stable: true, none of these was there, but it was very evident that this yard could not have been deserted long by its tenants. The house must, also, in my opinion, have been torn down, for of traces of fire, as, for example, charred beams, damaged stoves, and rubbish heaps, there was no sign.

In a word, it could be plainly perceived that the house which once stood there had been pulled down, and its beams and timbers carried away. In the middle of the premises, near the line hedge, stood several high trees, acacias, fig, and plum-trees; scattered among them were gooseberry bushes, rose-trees, and blackthorns, while near the street, just in the place where the window of the house was probably set, stood a high, green fig-tree.

I have seen many vacant lots, yet never before have I given a passing thought as to whom any one of them belonged, or who might have lived there, or indeed where its future possessor might be. But in a peculiar way the sight of this yard called up questions of this sort; and as I looked at it many different thoughts came into my mind. Perhaps, I thought to myself, a childless fellow, who spoiled old age with sighs and complaints, and as his life waned the walls moldered. Finally, the house was without a master; the doors and windows stood open, and when the dark winter nights came on, the neighbors fell upon it and stripped off its boards, one after another. Yes, various thoughts came into my head. How hard it is to build a house, and how easy to tear it down!

While I stood there lost in thought, an old woman, leaning on a staff, passed me. I did not immediately recognize her, but at a second glance I saw it was Hripsime.

Nurse Hripsime was a woman of five-and-seventy, yet, from her steady gait, her lively speech, and her fiery eyes, she appeared to be scarcely fifty. She was vigorous and hearty, expressed her opinions like a man, and was abrupt in her speech. Had she not worn women's garments one could easily have taken her for a man. Indeed, in conversation she held her own with ten men.

Once, I wot not for what reason, she was summoned to court. She went thither, placed herself before the judge, and spoke so bravely that everyone gaped and stared at her as at a prodigy. Another time thieves tried to get into her house at night, knowing that she was alone like an owl in the house. The thieves began to pry open the door with a crowbar, and when Nurse Hripsime heard it she sprang nimbly out of bed, seized her stick from its corner, and began to shout: "Ho, there! Simon, Gabriel, Matthew, Stephan, Aswadur, get up quickly. Get your axes and sticks. Thieves are here; collar the rascals; bind them, skin them, strike them dead!" The thieves probably did not know with whom they had to deal, and, when at the outcry of the old woman they conceived that a half-dozen stout-handed fellows might be in the house, they took themselves off. Just such a cunning, fearless woman was Aunt Hripsime.

"Good-morning, nurse," said I.

"God greet thee," she replied.

"Where have you been?"

"I have been with the sick," she rejoined.

Oh, yes! I had wholly forgotten to say that Nurse Hripsime, though she could neither read nor write, was a skilful physician. She laid the sick person on the grass, administered a sherbet, cured hemorrhoids and epilepsy; and especially with sick women was she successful. Yes, to her skill I myself can bear witness. About four years ago my child was taken ill in the dog-days, and for three years my wife had had a fever, so that she was very feeble. The daughter of Arutin, the gold-worker, and the wife of Saak, the tile-maker, said to me: "There is an excellent physician called Hripsime. Send for her, and you will not regret it." To speak candidly, I have never found much brains in our doctor. He turns round on his heels and scribbles out a great many prescriptions, but his skill is not worth a toadstool.

I sent for Hripsime, and, sure enough, not three days had passed before my wife's fever had ceased and my children's pain was allayed. For three years, thank God, no sickness has visited my house. Whether it can be laid to her skill and the lightness of her hand or to the medicine I know not. I know well, however, that Nurse Hripsime is my family physician. And what do I pay her? Five rubles a year, no more and no less. When she comes to us it is a holiday for my children, so sweetly does she speak to them and so well does she know how to win their hearts. Indeed, if I were a sultan, she should be my vezir.

"How does the city stand in regard to sickness?" I asked her.

"Of that one would rather not speak," answered Hripsime. "Ten more such years and our whole city will become a hospital. Heaven knows what kind of diseases they are! Moreover, they are of a very peculiar kind, and often the people die very suddenly. The bells fly in pieces almost from so much tolling, the grave-diggers' shovels are blunt, and from the great demand for coffins the price of wood is risen. What will become of us, I know not."

"Is not, then, the cause of these diseases known to you?"

"Oh, that is clear enough," answered Hripsime. "It is a punishment for our sins. What good deeds have we done that we should expect God's mercy? Thieves, counterfeiters, all these you find among us. They snatch the last shirt from the poor man's back, purloin trust moneys, church money: in a word, there is no shameless deed we will not undertake for profit. We need not wonder if God punishes us for it. Yes, God acts justly, praised be his holy name! Indeed, it would be marvelous if God let us go unpunished."

Hripsime was not a little excited, and that was just what I wished. When she once began she could no longer hold in: her words gushed forth as from a spring, and the more she spoke the smoother her speech.

"Do you know?" I began again, "that I have been standing a long while before this deserted yard, and cannot recall whose house stood here, why they have pulled it down, and what has become of its inhabitants? You are an aged woman, and have peeped into every corner of our city: you must have something to tell about it. If you have nothing important on hand, be kind enough to tell me what you know of the former residents of the vanished house."

Nurse Hripsime turned her gaze to the vacant yard, and, shaking her head, said:

"My dear son, the history of that house is as long as one of our fairy-tales. One must tell for seven days and seven nights in order to reach the end."

"This yard was not always so desolate as you see it now," she went on. "Once there stood here a house, not very large, but pretty and attractive, and made of wood. The wooden houses of former days pleased me much better than the present stone houses, which look like cheese mats outside and are prisons within. An old proverb says, 'In stone or brick houses life goes on sadly.'"

"Here, on this spot, next to the fig-tree," she continued, "stood formerly a house with a five-windowed front, green blinds, and a red roof. Farther back there by the acacias stood the stable, and between the house and the stable, the kitchen and the hen-house. Here to the right of the gate a spring." With these words Nurse Hripsime took a step forward, looked about, and said: "What is this? the spring gone, too! I recollect as if to-day that there was a spring of sweet water on the very spot where I am standing. What can have happened to it! I know that everything can be lost—but a spring, how can that be lost?" Hripsime stooped and began to scratch about with her stick. "Look here," she said suddenly, "bad boys have filled up the beautiful spring with earth and stones. Plague take it! Well, if one's head is cut off, he weeps not for his beard. For the spring I care not, but for poor Sarkis and his family I am very sorry."

"Are you certain that the house of Sarkis, the grocer, stood here? I had wholly forgotten it. Now tell me, I pray, what has become of him? Does he still live, or is he dead? Where is his family? I remember now that he had a pretty daughter and also a son."

Nurse Hripsime gave no heed to my questions, but stood silently, poking about with her stick near the choked-up spring.

The picture of Grocer Sarkis, as we called him, took form vividly in my memory, and with it awoke many experiences of my childhood. I remembered that when I was a child a dear old lady often visited us, who was continually telling us about Grocer Sarkis, and used to hold up his children as models. In summer, when the early fruit was ripe, she used to visit his house, gather fruit in his garden, and would always come to us with full pockets, bringing us egg-plums, saffron apples, fig-pears, and many other fruits. From that time we knew Sarkis, and when my mother wanted any little thing for the house I got it for her at his store. I loved him well, this Sarkis; he was a quiet, mild man, around whose mouth a smile hovered. "What do you want, my child?" he always asked when I entered his store.

"My mother sends you greeting," I would answer. "She wants this or that."

"Well, well, my child, you shall have it," he usually answered, and always gave me a stick of sugar candy, with the words, "That is for you; it is good for the cough." It never happened that I went out of the store without receiving something from him. In winter-time he treated me to sugar candy, and in summer-time he always had in his store great baskets full of apricots, plums, pears, and apples, or whatever was in season in his garden. His garden at that time—some thirty or thirty-five years ago—was very famous. One time my mother sent me to Sarkis's store to procure, as I remember, saffron for the pillau. Sarkis gave me what I desired, and then noticing, probably, how longingly I looked toward the fruit-baskets, he said:

"Now, you shall go and have a good time in my garden. Do you know where my house is?"

"Yes, I know. Not far from the Church of Our Lady."

"Right, my son, you have found it. It has green blinds, and a fig-tree stands in front of it. Now take this basket and carry it to Auntie, and say that I sent word that she was to let you go into the garden with my son Toros. There you two may eat what you will."

He handed me a neat-looking basket. I peeped into it and saw a sheep's liver. I was as disgusted with this as though it were a dead dog, for at that time liver-eaters were abhorred not less than thieves and counterfeiters; they with their whole family were held in derision, and people generally refused to associate with them. In a moment I forgot entirely what a good man Sarkis was; I forgot his fruit-garden and his pretty daughter, of whom the good old lady had told me so many beautiful things. The liver had spoiled everything in a trice. Sarkis noticed this, and asked me smiling:

"What is the matter?"

"Have you a dog in your yard?" I asked, without heeding his words.

"No," he said.

"For whom, then, is the liver?"

"For none other than ourselves. We will eat it."

I looked at Sarkis to see if he were jesting with me, but no sign of jesting was to be seen in his face.

"You will really eat the liver yourselves?" I asked.

"What astonishes you, my boy? Is not liver to be eaten, then?"

"Dogs eat liver," I said, deeply wounded, and turned away, for Sarkis appeared to me at that moment like a ghoul.

Just then there came into the store a pretty, pleasing boy. "Mamma sent me to get what you have bought at the Bazaar, and the hearth-fire has been lit a long time." I concluded that this was Sarkis's son, Toros. I perceived immediately from his face that he was a good boy, and I was very much taken with him.

"Here, little son, take that," Sarkis said, and handed him the basket which I had set down.

Toros peeped in, and when he spied the liver he said, "We will have a pie for dinner." Then he put on his cap and turned to go.

"Toros," called his father to him, "take Melkon with you to our house and play with him as a brother."

I was exceedingly pleased with the invitation, and went out with Toros. When we arrived at Sarkis' house and entered the garden it seemed as though I were in an entirely new world. The yard was very pretty, no disorder was to be seen anywhere. Here and there pretty chickens, geese, and turkeys ran about with their chicks. On the roof sat doves of the best kinds. The yard was shaded in places by pretty green trees, the house had a pretty balcony, and under the eaves stood green-painted tubs for catching rain-water. In the windows different flowers were growing, and from the balcony hung cages of goldfinches, nightingales, and canary birds; in a word, everything I saw was pretty, homelike, and pleasant.

In the kitchen cooking was going on, for thick smoke rose from the chimney. At the kitchen-door stood Sarkis's wife, a healthy, red-cheeked, and vigorous woman, apparently about thirty years old. From the fire that burned on the hearth her cheeks were still more reddened, so that it seemed, as they say, the redness sprang right out of her. On a little stool on the balcony sat a little girl, who wore, according to the prevailing fashion, a red satin fez on her head. This was Toros's sister. I have seen many beautiful girls in my time, but never a prettier one. Her name was Takusch.

Getting the mother's consent, we entered the garden, where we helped ourselves freely to the good fruit and enjoyed the fragrance of many flowers. At noon, Sarkis came home from the store, and invited me to dinner. My gaze was continually directed toward the beautiful Takusch. Oh, well-remembered years! What a pity it is that they pass by so quickly! Two or three months later I journeyed to the Black Sea, where I was apprenticed to a merchant, and since that time I have not been in my native city—for some twenty-four years—and all that I have told was awakened in my memory in a trice by my meeting with Hripsime.

The old woman was still standing on the site of the choked-up spring, scratching around on the ground with her stick.

"Nurse Hripsime, where is Sarkis and his family now?" I asked.

"Did you know him, then?" she asked, astonished.

"Yes, a little," I replied.

"Your parents were acquainted with him?"

"No. I was only once in his house, and then as a boy."

"Oh, then! That was his happiest time. What pleasant times we had in his garden! Formerly it was not as it is now—not a trace of their pleasant garden remains. The house has disappeared. Look again: yonder was the kitchen, there the hen-house, there the barn, and here the spring."

As she spoke she pointed out with her stick each place, but of the buildings she named not a trace was to be seen.

"Ah, my son," she went on, "he who destroyed the happiness of these good, pious people, who tore down their house and scattered the whole family to the winds, may that man be judged by God! He fell like a wolf upon their goods and chattels. I wish no evil to him, but if there is a God in heaven may he find no peace in his house, may his children bring no joy to him, and may no happiness find its way within his four walls. As he ruined those four poor wretches and was guilty of their early death, so may he roam over the wide world without rest nor find in sleep any comfort! Yes, may his trouble and sorrow increase with the abundance of his wealth!"

[Nurse Hripsime continues to tell the rest of the story.]

"I knew Sarkis when he was still a boy. When you knew him he must have been about forty years old. He was always just as you saw him: reserved, discreet, pious, beneficent to the poor, and hospitable. It never occurred that he spoke harshly to his wife or raised his hand against his children. He was ever satisfied with what he had; never complained that he had too little, or coveted the possessions of others. Yes, a pious man was Sarkis, and his wife had the same virtues. Early in childhood she lost her parents, and relatives of her mother adopted her, but treated her badly. Yes, bitter is the lot of the orphan, for even if they have means they are no better off than the poor! They said that when her father died he left her a store with goods worth about 3,000 rubles, and beside that 2,000 ducats in cash; but he was hardly dead when the relations came and secured the stock and gold as guardians of the orphan. When she was fourteen years old, one after another wooed her, but when the go-betweens found out that there was nothing left of her property they went away and let the girl alone."

"Happily for her, Sarkis appeared, and said: 'I want a wife; I seek no riches.' Of course, the relations gave her to him at once, and with her all sorts of trumpery, some half-ruined furniture, and a few gold pieces. 'That is all her father left', they said, and demanded from him a receipt for the whole legacy from her father. That was the way they shook her off! "

"At that time Sarkis himself had nothing, and was just as poor as his wife. He was clerk in a store, and received not more than 150 rubles in notes yearly, which were worth in current money scarcely one-third their face value. Yes, they were both poor, but God's mercy is great and no one can fathom his purposes! In the same year the merchant whom he served suddenly died after making over to Sarkis the whole store and all that was in it, on condition that a certain sum should be paid every year to the widow."

"Sarkis took the business, and after three years he was sole owner of it. He increased it continually, and on the plot of ground he had inherited from his father he built a pretty house and moved into it. In the same year God gave him a daughter, whom he named Takusch, and four years later his son Toros came into the world."

"So these two orphans established a household and became somebodies; people who had laughed at them now sought their society, and began to vie with each other in praising Sarkis. But Sarkis remained the same God-fearing Sarkis. He spoke evil of no one, and even of his wife's relatives, who had robbed him, he said nothing. Indeed, when they had gone through that inheritance and were in want he even helped them out."

"As I have said, Sarkis refused no one his assistance, but his wife had also a good heart. The good things she did cannot be told. How often she baked cracknel, cakes, rolls, and sweet biscuit, and sent great plates full of them to those who could not have such things, for she said, 'May those who pass by and smell the fragrance of my cakes never desire them in vain.' "

"About this time my husband died—may God bless him!—and I was living alone. Sarkis's wife came to me and said, 'Why will you live so lonely in your house? Rent it and come to us.' Of course, I did not hesitate long. I laid my things away in a large chest and moved over to their house, and soon we lived together like two sisters. Takusch was at that time four years old, and Toros was still a baby in arms. I lived ten years at their house, and heard not a single harsh word from them. Not once did they say to me, 'You eat our bread, you drink our water, you wear our clothing.' They never indulged in such talk: on the contrary, they placed me in the seat of honor. Yes, so they honored me. And, good heavens! what was I to them! Neither mother nor sister nor

33

aunt, in no way related to them. I was a stranger taken from the streets."

"Yes, such God-fearing people were Sarkis and his wife. The poor wretches believed that all mankind were as pure in heart as they were. I had even at that time a presentiment that they would not end well, and often remonstrated with them, begging them to be on their guard with people. But it was useless for me to talk, for they sang the old songs again."

"Like a sweet dream my years with the good people passed. Surely pure mother's milk had nourished them! I knew neither pain nor grief, nor did I think of what I should eat to-morrow, nor of how I could clothe myself. As bounteous as the hand of God was their house to me. Twelve months in every year I sat peacefully at my spinning-wheel and carried on my own business."

"Once during dog-days—Takusch was at that time fifteen years old and beginning her sixteenth year—toward evening, according to an old custom, we spread a carpet in the garden and placed a little table there for tea. Near us steamed and hissed the clean shining tea-urn, and around us roses and pinks shed their sweet odors. It was a beautiful evening, and it became more beautiful when the full moon rose in the heavens like a golden platter. I remember that evening as clearly as though it were yesterday. Takusch poured out the tea, and Auntie Mairam, Sarkis's wife, took a cup; but as she lifted it to her lips it fell out of her hand and the tea was spilled over her dress."

"My spirits fell when I saw this, for my heart told me that it meant something bad was coming. 'Keep away, evil; come, good,' I whispered, and crossed myself in silence. I glanced at Takusch and saw that the poor child had changed color. Then her innocent soul also felt that something evil was near! Sarkis and Mairam, however, remained in merry mood and thought of nothing of that sort. But if you believe not a thousand times that something is to come, it comes just the same! Mairam took her napkin and wiped off her dress and Takusch poured her a fresh cup. 'here will come a guest with a sweet tongue,' said Sarkis, smiling. 'Mairam, go and put another dress on. You will certainly be ashamed if anyone comes.' "

" 'Who can come to-day, so late?' said Mairam, smiling;' and, beside, the dress will dry quickly.' "

"Scarcely had she spoken when the garden door opened with a rush and a gentleman entered the enclosure. He had hardly stepped into the garden when he began to blab with his goat's voice like a windmill."

" 'Good-evening. How are you? You are drinking tea? That is very fine for you. What magnificent air you have here! Good-evening, Mr. Sarkis. Good-evening, Mrs. Mairam, Good-evening, Hripsime. What are you doing? I like to drink tea in the open air. What a beautiful garden you have. Dare I taste these cherries? Well—they are not bad; no, indeed, they are splendid cherries. If you will give me a napkin full of these cherries I will carry them home to my wife. And what magnificent apricots! Mr. Sarkis, do you know what! Sell me your house. No, I will say something better to you. Come to my store—you know where it is— yonder in the new two-storied house. Yes, yes, come over there and we will sit down pleasantly by the desk and gossip about Moscow happenings.' "

"We were as if turned to stone. There are in the world many kinds of madmen, chatterboxes, and braggarts, but such a creature as this I saw for the first time in my life, and do you know who it was? Hemorrhoid Jack."

"Have you heard of him? Have you seen this hostage of God?" Hripsime asked.

"No, I do not know him," I said.

"What! and you live in our city? Is there anyone who does not know the scoundrel? Go to the brokers, and they will tell you many he has thrown out of house and home by fraud and hunted out of the city. Have you ever seen how a bird-catcher lures the birds into his net—how he whistles to them? That's the way this John gets the people into his traps. To-day he will act as if altogether stupid. To-morrow he is suddenly shrewd, and understands the business well. Then he is simple again and a pure lamb. Now he is avaricious, now generous. And so he goes on. Yes, he slips around among the people like a fox with his tail wagging, and when he picks out his victim, he fastens his teeth in his neck and the poor beggar is lost. He gets him in his debt and never lets him get his breath between interest payments, or he robs him almost of his last shirt and lets him run. But see how I run away from my story!"

" 'Good-evening,' said Sarkis, as soon as he perceived Hemorrhoid Jack, and offered him his hand. 'What wind has blown you here? Mairam, a cup of tea for our honored Mr. John.' "

" 'Mr. Sarkis, do you know why I have come to you?' began Jack. 'The whole world is full of your praise; everywhere they are talking about you,' and I thought to myself, 'I must go there and see what kind of a man this Sarkis is.' And so here I am. Excuse my boldness. I cannot help it: I resemble in no way your stay-at-home. I am somewhat after the European fashion, you know. Who pleases me, I visit him quite simply. Present myself and make his acquaintance. Then I invite him to my house, go again to his and bring my family with me. Yes, such a fellow am I, let them laugh at me who will.' "

" 'Oh,' I thought, 'poor Sarkis is already fallen into the net, and his family with him.' "

"Meanwhile, Mairam had poured the tea, placed the cup on a tray, and Takusch had put it before Jack."

" 'Where did you buy the tea?' he began, taking the cup. 'When you want tea, buy it of me, I pray. You know, I am sure, where my store is. I can give you every desirable brand, and at low price. The tea that cost two rubles I will give to you for one ruble ninety-five kopecks. Yes, I will sell it to you at a loss. Oh, what bad tea you drink!' At the same time he began to sip and in a moment emptied the cup. 'Be so good as to give me another cup,' he said. 'In the fresh air one gets an appetite. If I am to enjoy tea-drinking, let me hitch up my carriage and drive out to the Monastery Gardens. There, out-of-doors, I drink two or three glasses and settle for them. Yes, such European customs please me.' "

"'May it benefit you!' said Sarkis."

"'Now, now, Mr. Sarkis, are you coming to my house to-morrow?' asked Hemorrhoid Jack."

" 'I will see,' answered Sarkis."

" 'What is there to see? If you want to come, come then. We will sit behind the counter, drink our glass of tea, and chat. Now and then, we will talk about European affairs, bookkeeping, news, and other things.' "

" 'All right, I shall surely come. I shall not forget.' "

" 'Good. And now it is time for me to be gone, for I must make two more visits to-day,' remarked Hemorrhoid Jack."

" 'Do they pay visits at this hour?' responded Sarkis. 'It must be nearly ten o'clock. Takusch, get a light.'"

"Takusch went into the room, and soon returned with a light. Sarkis took out his watch, and coming near the light said: 'Look, it is already a quarter to ten.' "

"John looked, and at once cried out: 'Oh, Mr. Sarkis, what a magnificent watch you have! Where did you get it? It appears to me to be a costly one. Let me see it.' "

" 'This watch I received as a gift from our late Czar. You know that several years ago our late Czar visited Taganrog. On this occasion the people of Taganrog wished to give him a magnificent horse, but they could not find an appropriate saddle. It happened that I had one that would do, and when they heard of it, they came to me and told me for what they needed the saddle. Who would not be ready to make such a sacrifice for the Czar? Indeed, who would not only sacrifice a costly saddle (and this one was not worth much), but even his life, gladly, if need be? Therefore, I immediately hired a wagon, and taking this extraordinary saddle with me and then on to Taganrog to the governor's.' "

" 'Your Highness seeks a saddle?' I asked."

" 'Yes, indeed,' he answered."

" 'Here it is,' said I."

" 'Thank you,' he said, and pressed my hand. Then he led me into his own room. By George! it looked like one in a king's castle. He had me sit down, served me with tea, invited me to dine at his table: in a word, he treated me well. At my departure, he took out of a drawer a ring set with genuine brilliants, gave it to me, and said, 'Take this from me as a gift, and what I receive from the Czar I will give to you also.' And he kept his word. The Czar really came, and they gave him the horse with my saddle. His Majesty thanked me for it and gave me this watch. 'Look, now, what a beautiful one it is!' "

" 'Yes, truly, it is a pretty thing. Show me it again. I

wish to see what kind of a watch it is,' said Hemorrhoid Jack, examining the watch. 'And have you the ring by you? Can I see it? Oh, let me see what kind of a thing it is. I like to see such things, particularly if they come from persons of high rank.' "

" 'Is the ring not in the chest of drawers?' said Sarkis, looking around toward his wife."

" 'Yes, I keep it there,' answered Mairam, faintly, for she might well foresee something evil. 'Who is it routs about in the chest of drawers in the night?' "

" 'Good Auntie Mairam,' began Jack, in a wheedling tone, 'I beg of you, bring the ring, that I may see it. Be so kind! When I see such a rare thing my heart leaps in my breast with delight. It is true joy for me to hold such things in my hand and look at them. Bring me the ring, I beg of you.' "

"I looked at him at that moment, and he seemed to me like a veritable gypsy. Had I not been obliged to consider those present, I should certainly have spit in his face, so great was my aversion to this scoundrel. Yes, what the proverb says is true: 'If a rich man becomes poor, he is scented for years with his wealth; if a poor man grows rich he stinks of poverty for forty years!' That was the way with this Hemorrhoid Jack. Oh, if it had been in my power I would have seized the scoundrel by the collar and thrown him out of the gate. But Sarkis was not of my temperament; he had a gentle heart and was meek as a lamb. I went up to him, pushed his elbow, and whispered:"

" 'What are you doing, you good-natured fool? Why did you let him take the watch in his hand? And are you going to show the ring, too? You will see, he has bad intentions. I'll bet my head he will bring misfortune on yours. Do you not see his greedy eyes? He will ruin you altogether, you and house, and ground,' I said."

"I had my trouble for my pains. Although a man of ripe years, Sarkis was nevertheless like a mere boy, believing all people as honest as himself. Heaven knows! perhaps such a fate was destined for him, and it was impossible for him to get out of the way of misfortune."

"Mairam brought the ring, and as soon as the

38

scoundrel saw it he grabbed it from her hand and put it on his finger."

" 'What a pretty thing it is!' he said, smirking. 'How it glistens! What a precious ring! What wonderfully beautiful brilliants! What ought I to give you for such a ring? Tell me. It pleases me exceedingly. Yes, without joking, sell it to me. No, we will arrange it otherwise: I will give you all kinds of goods out of my store at a very low price, yes, very cheap. May the apoplexy strike me if I make anything out of you! I will sell you everything at cost price, and if you wish, will give you ten kopecks rebate on the ruble.' "

" 'No, my dear sir', said Mairam, embarrassed. 'Can one sell a souvenir of the Czar, and one of such great value? We have no occasion to do it. We are no Jews, to sell off everything, to turn into money whatever comes into our hands. Are we such poor beggars that we cannot have something good and valuable in our chest? No, Mr. John, what you say seems to me to be very singular. You are rich, yet you say that you have never in your life seen a gold watch nor a ring set with brilliants. It seems to me a fine new custom that one must immediately have what one sees. No, dear sir, cast not your eyes upon our property; be content with what you have.' "

" 'Mrs. Mairam,' said the scoundrel, smirking, 'why are you so angry? May one not joke with you?' "

" 'A fine joke!' I said, putting in my oar. 'You looked at the trees, and you will at once tear them down. You fell on the fruit like a wolf. You saw the garden, and at once wanted to buy. Now you want the ring, and will exchange for it your wares. What sort of tomfoolery are you talking to us? You are either crazy yourself or will make others so. The apple falls not far from the stem—one sees that in you.' "

" 'Aunt Hripsime, why are you so cross? Dare one not jest?' "

" 'Enough, enough; I understand your joke very well, I cried indignantly.' "

"Yes, we women scolded him right well, but Sarkis said no earthly word. He sat there dumb and speechless as the stick in my hand. The Lord God gave him a tongue to speak with, but, dear heaven, he sat there like a clod and never uttered a syllable. I was like to burst with wrath."

"Then that unscrupulous fellow repeated his speech. 'Don't you understand a joke? Have you, then, no sense of fun?' He would have struck us over the ear, and that the fellow called a joke! And how the creature looked! His face was like a drum-skin. It was as though someone had wiped off the holy oil from this grimacing mask with a butcher's sponge. Yes, here you see how people become rich; how they get hold of other people's property. Conscience hunts the scoundrel to the deuce: he lets his skin grow thick; feigns outwardly to be dull; if anyone spits in his face he regards it only as a May-shower; if anyone goes for him for his rascality, he takes it as a joke. And so the rascals become rich! One must be born to those things, that's the way I see it.' "

"If you knew all that we said to this scoundrel's face! We all but seized him by the collar and threw him out the gate. We belabored him well, but the fellow stood as if dumb, remained silent, and laughed in our faces as if we had been speaking to each other and not to him. He neither took the watch out of his pocket nor the ring from his finger. Finally, I thought to myself, 'I will wait a little and see what will happen.' "

"And do you know what this bad fellow said to our Sarkis after a short silence? 'Your watch and ring please me well, old fellow. Let me take them for a month or two. I will send them to Moscow and have some like them made for myself. As soon as I get them back I will give them back to you unhurt.' "

"Our stupid Sarkis dared not say no, and he had his way."

" 'Take them,' said Sarkis, 'but take care that they do not go astray, for—' "

" 'But what are you thinking about?' answered the scoundrel. 'Am I then—. Where do you buy your calico?' the scoundrel began after a pause. 'How much do you pay an ell? Where do you buy your linen cloth? How high does it come by the ell? Where do you buy your silk and satin?' "

"Heaven knows what all he prated about, and Sarkis answered him and told everything just as it really was."

" 'We buy our manufactured goods of Yellow Pogos,' and told the prices of everything without reserve."

" 'Have you lost your wits, man?' cried Hemorrhoid Jack. 'Can any man in his full senses buy anything of Yellow Pogos? Don't you know that he is a swindler? Why don't you buy your goods of me? I will give them to you cheaper by half.' "

"To this Sarkis answered, 'When I need something again I will buy it of you.' "

"I knew well enough that Sarkis needed nothing at the time, and that he said this only to get rid of the fellow. But Jack did not or would not understand, and began again."

" 'No, do not put it that way,' he said. 'Come to-morrow and pick out what pleases you. Do not think for a minute that I wish to make money out of you. Let the goods lie in your closet, for, between ourselves, goods were very cheap in Moscow this year, and I cleverly threw out my line and bought everything at half price. This year is a lucky one for my customers. If one of them will let his goods lie a little while he will certainly double his money on them. Yes, buy, I tell you, but not by the ell. Buy by the piece and you will not regret it, I assure you. I will send you in the morning five or six different kinds of goods.' "

" 'But why such haste?' said Mairam. 'My chest of drawers is full of stuff for clothes, and what I am wearing is still quite new. If we need anything we will come to you.' "

" 'What are you talking about, Auntie Mairam?' answered Hemorrhoid Jack. 'Do you not believe me? I tell you, you can get double for the goods, and if you cannot use everything yourself, give it to your neighbors. You will do good business. On my word of honor, I swear to you, you will make double on it. Would I lie for the sake of such a trifle? Whom do you think you have here? But that is a small matter: I have still something better to propose. You must take a shipment of tea from me. In the winter the price will rise, and you can make enormous profits out of it. To-morrow I will send you one chest—for the present. Well? Now, really, I will send it to you.' "

" 'My dear John,' exclaimed Sarkis, 'you must know how risky it is to begin a new business. I have never handled tea, and the thing appears to me somewhat daring. I know no customers for tea, and understand nothing about the goods. If it remains lying by me and spoils—' "

" 'What empty straw are you threshing now?' cried Hemorrhoid Jack. 'As soon as the people know that you have tea to sell they will of their own accord come running into your store. Do you think that you will have to look up customers? In a week or two not a trace of your tea will remain. I speak from practical experience. This year little tea has been brought from Siberia, and what they have brought has almost all fallen into my hands. Do not think that I seek a buyer in you! God forbid! When I learned what a good man you were, I thought to myself, 'I must give him a chance to make something. Yes, I want him to make a few kopecks' Do you think I am in need of purchasers? Now, Sarkis, to-morrow I will send you the goods. What?' "

" 'By heaven, I know not how I ought to answer you. Do you know, I am afraid,' said Sarkis."

"The poor fellow could say nothing farther, for he was such an honest, good-natured fellow that it was hard for him to refuse anybody anything. The word 'no' did not exist for him."

" 'You are talking nonsense,' began Hemorrhoid Jack anew. 'Give up your grocery and set up a wholesale business. Manage it according to the European plan, and you shall see how thankful to me you will be in time. Do you believe that I am your enemy? Would I advise you badly? Now, the matter is settled. In the morning I will send you several chests of tea and put them in your store. You will find out that Hemorrhoid Jack wishes you no ill. Yes, I will say something even better. You know what machorka is?—a cheap tobacco that the poor folk smoke. What do you think of this stuff? Do you think that there is a class of goods more profitable than this? People make thousands from it, and build themselves fine houses. And what expenses have they with it? Put the tobacco in an empty stable or shed and it may lie there. A chest of it put on sale in your store and I tell you, if you do not make ruble for ruble out of it, then spit in my face.' "

" 'Last spring most of this stuff was in the hands of a Cossack. The stupid fellow didn't know what he ought to expect for it, and he needed money—this gander! I brought him home with me; had brandy, bread, and ham set out; and, after a little talk back and forth, I bought 400 chests at half price. Half I paid in cash, the rest in eighteen months.

42

Now, wasn't that a good trade? If I don't make my 3,000 rubles out of it, I shall be a fool. If you like, I will send you some of these goods. Put it in your shop or in your shed and let it lie there; it eats and drinks nothing. Now, I tell you, if you do not make 100 per cent, out of it, spit in my face. Shall I send you a few chests of it?' "

" 'By heaven, I cannot go into it,' answered Sarkis. 'Do you know, I am afraid to undertake a new trade? If the stuff does not go off or spoils on my hands or the price falls, what shall I do? You know that our capital consists of only a few kopecks. We spend as we earn. If I run after the rubles and lose the kopecks thereby, who will give me something to eat?' concluded the poor wretch, as if he scented some evil."

"But could he free himself from that Satan of a Hemorrhoid Jack? Like a leech he had fastened himself on his neck and demanded that he should buy the goods."

" 'Now, Sarkis,' he began again, 'the thing is settled. I am to send you in the morning manufactured goods, tea, and tobacco. Well?' "

" 'I will see; I must turn it over in my mind,' stammered Sarkis. He wanted to be rid of him, but he knew not how to begin. "

" 'What does that I will see! mean?' 'Nothing,' the other continued. 'You may see a thousand times and you will not find again such good goods and such a favorable opportunity. I speak from experience. You must not let this chance slip by or you will throw gold out of the window with your own hands. I am talking about great gains, great profits; do you think it is a joke?' "

" 'We shall see,' said poor Sarkis. 'We have many days before us. Yes, we will surely do something.' "

" 'What you do now is not worth much,' cried Hemorrhoid Jack. 'I see that if I leave the thing to your decision, in five years you will not have reached one. Isn't that true? In the morning I will send you one load of goods and the rest later.' "

"With these words he seized his cap, quickly made his adieus, and went away."

"It was nearly one o'clock; Mairam and Takusch were sitting there asleep and I also was very sleepy, but I fought against my sleepiness to watch that devil of a

Hemorrhoid Jack. Mankind can be a priest to mankind—also a Satan!"

"When he was in the street, Sarkis said to me: 'What a wonderful conversation we have had this evening. Of all this man has said, I understand nothing. His purposes are not exactly bad, but I don't know how it happens—my heart presages something of evil.' "

"I was just going to answer him when suddenly I sneezed; but only once."

" 'See now,' I said to Sarkis; 'I was right in saying he was going to trick you. Now it has proved itself.' "

" 'If one sneezes only once by day that is a bad sign, but at night it means something good,' he interrupted me."

" 'Oh,' I said, 'do not, I pray, give me lessons; don't teach me what a sneeze is the sign of. Whether it is in the daytime or at night it is a bad sign, and if one just made up his mind to do anything, he should let it
    drop.' "

"Sarkis would not give in that I was right, but began to chatter about a sneeze at night being a good thing. I said no and he said yes, and so it went on until I finally gave it up."

" 'Oh,' I said, 'have your own way, but when misfortune comes to you do not blame me for it.' "

" 'I have really begun nothing,' he observed. 'That was only a talk. We have only discussed something. I have really no desire to try my hand with the tea and tobacco.' "

"That he said to me, but heaven only knows! perhaps in his thoughts he was already counting the thousands he hoped to earn. Money has such power that my blessed grandmother always said that the devil had invented it. He had racked his brains to find a way to lead mankind into wickedness and did not succeed until he invented money. Then he was master of our souls. How many men money has deprived of reason! Sarkis was not of so firm a mind that he would be able to stand out against such rosy hopes."

"The next day, early in the morning, the shop-boy came running into the house in a great hurry, and said that nine cart-loads of goods were standing at the gate. The man who was in charge of them was asking for Sarkis."

" 'What kind of an invasion is this!' cried Sarkis. 'I

must go and see who it is. Perhaps the loads are not for me at all. God knows for whom they are!' "

"He went out, and we after him. Although I had not seen the loads of goods, I knew the whole story in a moment."

"Before we had reached the gate a man met us and said: 'My master sends you greeting and begs you to take these nine wagon-loads of goods and sign for them.' "

" 'Who is your master?' we asked, all together."

" 'Hemorrhoid Jack. Don't you know him? He was at your house last evening.' "

"I was ready to burst with anger."

" 'You fellow,' I said, 'who told your master to send these goods here? Have we ordered anything? Turn at once and get out of the room.' "

" 'Is that so!' said the man. 'After a thing is settled you can't take back your word. Where shall I put the goods now?' "

" 'Where you brought them from, take them back there!' "

" 'The coach-house is closed.' "

" 'That does not concern us; that is your master's affair.' "

" 'If he were here I would tell him, but he is not here.' "

" 'Where is he then?' I asked."

" 'He has gone to Taganrog.' "

" 'When did he start?' "

" 'About two hours ago. He will not be back for two months, for he has very important business in the courts.' "

"It could not be doubted now that this villain of a John had already begun his tricks; but that innocent Sarkis did not see through his devilish purposes. Had I been in his place I would have run immediately to the City Hall and told every detail of the business, and the thing would have come out all right. But Sarkis was not the man for that."

" 'Well, if that is the case drive into the yard and unload. The goods cannot stand in the street. When Jack comes back from Taganrog I will arrange things with him in some way.' "

"The wagons came into the yard with a clatter and the driver unloaded the goods and piled them up in the coach-house. I stood as if turned to stone and silently watched this move in their game. 'What will come of it?' I thought to myself."

"Ah, but I would rather have died than see what did come of it!"

"When the goods were unloaded the clerk demanded a receipt, which Sarkis gave him without hesitation, whereupon the clerk went away satisfied."

"Later we heard that Jack had not gone to Taganrog at all, and had only ordered the clerk to say so."

"That same day when we were sitting at dinner, Sarkis turned to me and said: 'See, Hripsime, your sneeze has cheated you. Did you not say that Jack was going to play a trick on me? You see something very different has happened. This forenoon four or five persons came into my shop who wished to buy tea and tobacco. I told them the matter was not yet settled; that we had not agreed on the price; as soon as the agreement was made I would begin business. Do you see? I have not advertised that I was going to handle the goods, yet everybody knows it and one customer after another comes into my store. How will it be when the goods are put on sale?—they will fight for them. It will give me a great deal to do; I must only go to John and settle on the terms. Yes, little mother, such a wholesale trade is not to be despised; the wholesaler can often make more money in a moment than the retailer makes in two years. Yes, my love, in business that is really so!' "

" 'God grant that it may be so!' I said, and nothing more was said about Jack."

"Several months passed by and November came. One evening we were sitting together chatting comfortably when the door opened softly and an old woman entered. I knew immediately that she was a matchmaker. In three days Takusch was betrothed to a plain, middle-rate man. The wedding was to take place the next winter on her father's name-day. As a dowry her parents promised 3,000 rubles—1,500 in cash, and the rest in jewels."

"Tagusch was at that time fifteen years old. Although I had lived in her parents' house I had never looked right attentively at her face, scarcely knew, in fact, whether she was beautiful or ugly; but when on her betrothal day she put on a silk dress and adorned herself as is customary at such a festive time; when she had put on her head a satin fez with gold tassels and a flower set with brilliants, I fairly gaped with admiration. I am almost eighty years old, but in all my life I have never seen a more beautiful girl."

"I am no dwarf, but she was a few inches taller than I. She was slender as a sweet-pine tree. Her hands were delicate and soft, her fingers were like wax. Hair and eyebrows were black, and her face like snow. Her cheeks were tinged rose-red, and her glance! that I cannot forget even to this day. It was brighter than a genuine Holland diamond. Her eyelashes were so long that they cast shadows on her cheeks. No, such a charming creature I have never seen in dreams, let alone reality. She was—God forgive my sins—the pure image of the Mother of God in our church; yes, she was even more beautiful. When I looked at her I could not turn my eyes away again. I gazed at her and could not look enough. On the betrothal day I sat in the corner of the room with my eyes nailed on Takusch."

" 'How sorry I am,' thought I, 'that you with that angel face are to be the wife of a commonplace man, to be the mother of a family and go into a dirty, smoky kitchen. Shall your tender hands become hard as leather with washing, ironing, kneading, and who knows what housework beside? Shall your angel cheeks fade from the heat of the oven and your eyes lose their diamond-shine from sewing?' Yes, so thought I, and my heart bled within me for this girl who ought to wear a queen's crown and live in a palace. Surely, if this rose maiden had lived in olden times she would certainly have married a king or a king's son. And the poor thing stood there like a lamb, for she did not understand what life was. She thought marriage would be nothing more than a change in her dwelling-place. Oh, but I was sorry that evening that she was going to marry only an ordinary, but still eligible, young man, and yet it would have been a great good fortune for her if this had come to pass. Had we thought at that time that great misfortunes were in store for the poor child! And that cursed Hemorrhoid Jack was the cause of them all!"

"That betrothal day was the last happy day of the poor wretches. I never afterward saw smiles on their faces, for

47

from that day their circumstances grew worse and worse and their business became very bad. They lost house and ground, moved about for several months from one rented house to another, until finally they disappeared from the city."

"The day after the betrothal Hemorrhoid Jack sent word to Sarkis by his clerk that Sarkis must pay 2,700 rubles for the tobacco and tea and 184 rubles for the manufactured goods. I have forgotten to tell you that among the latter were old-fashioned dress-goods, taxed cloth, linen, satin, and some silk. The clerk also said that if Sarkis did not pay the 184 rubles the ring and watch would be retained."

"Poor Sarkis was completely dazed."

" 'Have I bought the goods?' he asked."

" 'Certainly you have bought them,' answered the unscrupulous clerk. 'Otherwise you would not have sold a chest of tea and a bale of tobacco. Beside, the coat your boy is wearing was made from our cloth.' "

"This was true. On the third day after receiving the goods, Sarkis had sold a bale of tobacco and a chest of tea, and had cut off several yards of cloth. It was very singular that in the course of three months Sarkis had not once caught sight of Hemorrhoid Jack to call him to account for the delivery of the goods. He had been several times to his house, where they said, 'He is at the store.' At the store they said Jack was at home. It was very evident that he wished to defraud Sarkis. After much talk back and forth the matter came into the courts, and since Sarkis had sold part of the goods and had given a receipt for them, he had to pay the sum demanded."

"For several months past business had been going very badly with the poor fellow and he could not raise the required sum, so he had to give up his property. First they drove the poor man out of his house and emptied his store and his storehouse. Then they sold the tobacco and the tea, for which no one would give more than fifty rubles, for both were half rotten. The store and all that was in it were then auctioned off for a few hundred rubles, and finally the house was offered for sale. No one would buy it, for among our people the praiseworthy custom rules that they never buy a house put up at auction till they convince themselves that the owner sells it of his own free-will. The household furniture was also sold, and Sarkis became almost a beggar, and was obliged, half naked, to leave his house, with his wife and children."

"I proposed that they should occupy my house, but he would not have it. 'From to-day the black earth is my dwelling-place,' he said, and rented a small house at the edge of the town near where the fields begin."

"When the neighbors found out the treachery of Hemorrhoid Jack, they were terribly angry, and one of them threw a note into his yard in which was written: that if he took possession of poor Sarkis's house they would tear or burn it down. That was just what John wished, and he immediately sent carpenters to tear down the house and stable and then he sold the wood."

"At this time I became very sick and lay two months in bed. When I got up again I thought to myself, 'I must go and visit the poor wretches!' I went to their little house, but found the door locked and the windows boarded up. I asked a boy, "My child, do you know where the people of this house are?" "Two weeks ago they got into a wagon and drove away,' answered the lad. 'Where are they gone?' I asked. 'That I don't know,' he said."

"I would not have believed it, but an old woman came up to me on the street, of her own accord, and said: 'They all got into a wagon and have moved away into a Russian village.' "

"What the village was called she could not tell me, and so every trace of them was lost."

"Many years later a gentleman came from Stavropol to our city, who gave me some news of the poor wretches. They had settled in a Cossack village—he told me the name, but I have forgotten—where at first they suffered great want; and just as things were going a little better with them, Mairam and Sarkis died of the cholera and Takusch and Toros were left alone. Soon after, a Russian officer saw Takusch and was greatly pleased with her. After a few months she married him. Toros carried on his father's business for a time, then gave it up and joined the army. So much I found out from the gentleman from Stavropol."

"Some time later I met again one who knew Takusch. He told me that she was now a widow. Her husband had been a drunkard, spent his whole nights in inns, often struck his poor wife, and treated her very badly. Finally they brought him home dead. Toros's neck had been broken at a horse-race and he was dead. He said also that Takusch had almost forgotten the Armenian language and had changed her faith."

" 'That is the history of the Vacant Yard.' "

ARMENIAN POEMS
[Metrical Version, by Robert Arnot, M.A.]

A PLAINT

Were I a springtime breeze,
A breeze in the time when the song-birds pair,
I'd tenderly smooth and caress your hair,
And hide from your eyes in the budding trees.

Were I a June-time rose,
I'd glow in the ardor of summer's behest,
And die in my passion upon your breast,
In the passion that only a lover knows.

Were I a lilting bird,
I'd fly with my song and my joy and my pain,
And beat at your lattice like summer-rain,
Till I knew that your inmost heart was stirred.

Were I a winged dream,
I'd steal in the night to your slumbering side,
And the joys of hope in your bosom I'd hide,
And pass on my way like a murmuring stream.

Tell me the truth, the truth,
Have I merited woe at your tapering hands,
Have you wilfully burst love's twining strands,
And cast to the winds affection and ruth?

'Twas a fleeting vision of joy,
While you loved me you plumed your silvery wings,
And in fear of the pain that a man's love brings
You fled to a bliss that has no alloy.

Mugurditch Beshettashian

SPRING IN EXILE

Wind of the morn, of the morn of the year,
Violet-laden breath of spring,
To the flowers and the lasses whispering
Things that a man's ear cannot hear,
In thy friendly grasp I would lay my hand,
But thou comest not from my native land.

Birds of the morn, of the morn of the year,
Chanting your lays in the bosky dell,
Higher and fuller your round notes swell,
Till the Fauns and the Dryads peer forth to hear
The trilling lays of your feathery band:
Ye came not, alas, from my native land.

Brook of the morn, of the morn of the year,
Burbling joyfully on your way,
Maiden and rose and woodland fay
Use as a mirror your waters clear:
But I mourn as upon your banks I stand,
That you come not, alas, from my native land.

Breezes and birds and brooks of the Spring,
Chanting your lays in the morn of the year,
Though Armenia, my country, be wasted and sere,
And mourns for her maidens who never shall sing,
Yet a storm, did it come from that desolate land,
Would awaken a joy that ye cannot command.

Raphael Patkanian

FLY, LAYS OF MINE!

Fly, lays of mine, but not to any clime
Where happiness and light and love prevail,
But seek the spots where woe and ill and crime
Leave as they pass a noisome serpent-trail

Fly, lays of mine, but not to the ether blue,
Where golden sparks illume the heavenly sphere,
But seek the depths where nothing that is true
Relieves the eye or glads a listening ear.

Fly, lays of mine, but not to fruitful plains
Where spring the harvests by God's benison,
But seek the deserts where for needed rains
Both prayers and curses rise in unison.

Fly, lays of mine, but not to riotous halls,
Where dancing sylphs supply voluptuous songs,
But seek the huts where pestilence appals,
And death completes the round of human wrongs.

Fly, lays of mine, but not to happy wives,
Whose days are one unending flow of bliss,
But seek the maidens whose unfruitful lives
Have known as yet no lover's passionate kiss.

Fly, lays of mine, and like the nightingales,
Whose liquid liltings charm away the night,
Reveal in song the sweets of summer's gales,
Of lover's pleadings and of love's delight.

And tell my lady, when your quests are o'er,
That I, away from her, my heart's desire,
Yearn for the blissful hour when I shall pour
Down at her feet a love surcharged with fire.

Mugurditch Beshettashian

THE WOE OF ARAXES

Meditating by Araxes,
Pacing slowly to and fro,
Sought I traces of the grandeur
Hidden by her turgid flow.

Turgid are thy waters, Mother,
As they beat upon the shore.
Do they offer lamentations
For Armenia evermore?

Gay should be thy mood, O Mother,
As the sturgeons leap in glee:
Ocean's merging still is distant,
Shouldest thou be sad, like me?

Are thy spume-drifts tears, O Mother,
Tears for those that are no more?
Dost thou haste to pass by, weeping,
This thine own beloved shore?

Then uprose on high Araxes,
Flung in air her spumy wave,
And from out her depths maternal
Sonorous her answer gave:

"Why disturb me now, presumptuous,
All my slumbering woe to wake?
Why invade the eternal silence
For a foolish question's sake?

Know'st thou not that I am widowed;
Sons and daughters, consort, dead?
Wouldst thou have me go rejoicing,
As a bride to nuptial bed?

Wouldst thou have me decked in splendor,
To rejoice a stranger's sight,
While the aliens that haunt me
Bring me loathing, not delight?

Traitress never I; Armenia
Claims me ever as her own;
Since her mighty doom hath fallen
Never stranger have I known.

Yet the glories of my nuptials
Heavy lie upon my soul;
Once again I see the splendor
And I hear the music roll.

Hear again the cries of children
Ringing joyfully on my banks,
And the noise of marts and toilers,
And the tread of serried ranks.

But where, now, are all my people?
Far in exile, homeless, lorn.
While in widow's weeds and hopeless,
Weeping, sit I here and mourn.

Hear now! while my sons are absent
Age-long fast I still shall keep;
Till my children gain deliverance,
Here I watch and pray and weep."

Silent, then, the mighty Mother
Let her swelling tides go free.
And in mournful meditation
Slowly wandered to the sea.

Raphael Patkanian

THE ARMENIAN MAIDEN

In the hush of the spring night dreaming
The crescent moon have you seen,
As it shimmers on apricots gleaming,
Through velvety masses of green.

Have you seen, in a June-tide nooning,
A languorous full-blown rose
In the arms of the lilies swooning
And yielding her sweets to her foes?

Yet the moon in its course and the roses
By Armenia's maiden pale,
When she coyly and slowly discloses
The glories beneath her veil.

And a lute from her mother receiving,
With a blush that a miser would move,
She treads a soft measure, believing
That music is sister to love.

Like a sapling her form in its swaying,
Full of slender and lissomy grace
As she bends to the time of her playing,
Or glides with a fairy-light pace.

The lads for her beauty are burning,
The elders hold forth on old age,
But the maiden flies merrily spurning
Youth, lover, and matron and sage.

Raphael Patkanian

ONE OF A THOUSAND

Sweet lady, whence the sadness in your face?
What heart's desire is still unsatisfied?
Your face and form are fair and full of grace,
And silk and velvet lend you all their pride.
A nod, a glance, and straight your maidens fly
To execute your hest with loving zeal.
By night and day you have your minstrelsy,
Your feet soft carpets kiss and half conceal;
While fragrant blooms adorn your scented bower,
Fruits fresh and rare lie in abundance near.
The costly narghilé exerts its power
To soothe vain longing and dispel all fear:
Envy not angels; you have paradise.
No lowly consort you. A favored wife,
Whose mighty husband can her wants suffice;
Why mar with grieving such a fortunate life?

So to Haripsime, the Armenian maid,
On whom the cruel fortune of her lot had laid
Rejection of her faith, spake with a sigh
The wrinkled, ugly, haggard slave near by.

Haripsime replied not to the words,
But, silent, turned her face away. With scorn
And sorrow mingled were the swelling chords
Of passionate lament, and then forlorn,
Hopeless, she raised her tearful orbs to heaven.

Silent her lips, her grief too deep for sound;
Her fixed gaze sought the heavy banks of cloud
Surcharged with lightning bolts that played around
The gloomy spires and minarets; then bowed
Her head upon her hands; the unwilling eyes
Shed tears as heavy as the thunder-shower
That trails the bolt to where destruction lies.

There was a time when she, a happy girl,
Had home and parents and a numerous kin;
But on an Eastertide, amid a whirl

57

Of pillage, murder, and the savage din
Of plundering Kavasses, the Pacha saw
Her budding beauty, and his will was law.

Her vengeful sire fell 'neath a sabre's stroke;
Her mother, broken-hearted, gave to God
The life in which no joys could now evoke
The wonted happiness. The harem of the Turk
Enfolds Haripsime's fresh maidenhood,
And there where danger and corruption lurk,
Where Shitan's nameless and befouling brood
Surround each Georgian and Armenian pearl,
She weeps and weeps, shunning the shallow joys
Of trinkets, robes, of music, or the whirl
Of joyous dance, of singing girls and boys,
And murmurs always in a sobbing prayer,
"Shall never help be sent? Is this despair?"

Raphael Patkanian

LONGING

Tell me, brother, where is rest
From the flame that racks my breast
With its pain?
Fires unceasing sear my heart;
Ah, too long, too deep, the smart
To heal again.

When I'd pluck the roses sweet
Sharpest thorns my fingers greet;
Courage flies.
Since my love has humbled me,
Tyrant-like has troubled me,
'Spite my cries.
Health and joy have taken flight,
Prayer nor chant nor priestly rite
Do I prize.

Girl, my girl, my peerless one,
Radiant as Armenia's sun,
Beautiful Sanan!
Earth has none as fair as thou,
Nor can ages gone bestow
One like my Sanan.

Sixteen summers old is she,
Grace of slender pines has she,
Like the stars her eyes.
Lips, thrice blessed whom they kiss,
Brows as dark as hell's abyss,
And with sighs,
Her heart to win, her love alone,
What mighty prince from his high throne
Would not descend?
So I crave nor crown nor gold,
Longed-for One, I her would hold
Till time shall end.

Raphael Patkanian

DAVID OF SASSUN

NATIONAL EPOS OF ARMENIA
[*Translated by F.B. Collins, B.S.*]

Strong and mighty was the Caliph of Bagdad [1] ; he gathered together a host and marched against our Holy John the Baptist [2] . Hard he oppressed our people, and led many into captivity. Among the captives was a beautiful maiden, and the caliph made her his wife. In time she bore two sons, Sanassar and Abamelik. The father of these children was a heathen, but their mother was a worshipper of the cross [3] , for the caliph had taken her from our people.

This same caliph again gathered together a host and fell upon our people. This time—I bow before thy holy miracle, O sainted John—this time our people pressed him sorely, and in his affliction he cried unto his idols: "May the gods save me from these people; bring me to my city safe and well, and both my sons will I sacrifice unto them."

In Bagdad the mother lay sleeping, and she had a dream. She dreamed she had in each hand a lamp, and when their flames seemed ready to go out they flashed up brightly again. When morning came she told this dream to her sons, and said: "Last night holy St. John appeared to me in my

---

[1] From the sense and according to the time in which the action takes place, Nineveh must be understood here; and instead of an Arabian caliph, the Assyrian king Sennacherib. There is an anachronism here, as the reader will see, for a king living 800 years before Christ is called an Arabian caliph, though the caliphs first took up their residence in Bagdad in the year 755.

[2] The reference here is to the famous monastery of St. John the Baptist, which was built by Gregory the Illuminator during the fourth century, on the mountain of Kark, near the Euphrates, on a spot where heathen altars had previously stood. On certain days pious Armenians made annual pilgrimages to the place. Among them many poets and champions, who, with long fasts and many prayers, begged from the saint the gifts of song, strength, and courage. John the Baptist was regarded by the Armenians generally as the protector of the arts.

[3] So the Armenians called Christians.

dreams and said that your father was in great trouble and had vowed to sacrifice you. When he again comes home he will stab you: look to your safety."

Both sons cried unto their gods, took food with them for their journey, put gold into their purses, and set out on their travels. Coming to a narrow valley they halted there. They saw a river, and in the distance a brook clove the river to mid-stream, then mingled with its waters and flowed onward with it.

And Sanassar said to Abamelik: "He who finds the source of this brook and builds him a dwelling there, his race shall also wax mighty."

The brothers rose with one will and followed the brook upstream. They found its spring and saw its waters flowing as from a small pipe, and they ran down with the brook and increased till they mixed with waters of the great river. Here the brothers halted and laid the foundations of their dwelling.

And Sanassar hunted while Abamelik worked on the house. Ten, yea, twenty days they worked on their dwelling. It happened that once Abamelik came upon Sanassar asleep, worn out with fatigue, his venison thrown away unroasted. Abamelik was much troubled at this, and said, "Rise, brother, and we will depart from this place. How long shall we stay here and eat meat without salt? If it were God's will that we should have happiness, in our father's wooden palace we should have found it." And they mounted their horses and rode to the Lord of Arsrom. 4 Both came thither, presented themselves to him, and bowed before him.

Now both brothers were mighty men. They found favor with the Emir of Arsrom, and he asked them of their birth and of their tribe, and said, "What manner of men are you?"

Sanassar answered and said, "We are the sons of the Caliph of Bagdad."

---

4 The original name of this city is Theodosiopol. It was founded by the Greek commander Anato in the year 412 A.D. and named in honor of Emperor Theodosius II. Later it was captured by the Sultan of Ikonika, Who named it Arsi-Rom, "Land of the Greeks." The Armenians call it Karin, after the old Armenian province in which it lies.

"Hoho!" said the Emir, while terror seized him. "We feared you dead, and here we meet you living. We cannot take you in. Go whither ye will."

And Sanassar said to Abamelik, "Since we have run away from our father, why should we bear his name? From this day, when anyone asks us concerning ourselves, let us say we have neither father nor mother nor home nor country: then will people lodge us."

Thence they rode to the Emir of Kars, who gave the lads the same answer. They turned and rode to the King of Kraput-Koch. The King of Kraput-Koch scrutinized the lads, and they found favor in his sight; and Abamelik presented himself to the King and bowed low before him. This pleased the King greatly, and he said: "My children, whither came ye? What have you? and what do you lack?" [5]

"We have neither father nor mother nor anyone beside," answered the brothers.

And it came to pass that Sanassar became the King's *tschubuktschi* [6] and Abamelik his *haiwatschi,* [7] and they lived at the King's house a long time.

But Sanassar said one day to Abamelik: "We fatigued ourselves greatly with labor, yet was our house not finished. To-morrow make the King no coffee, nor will I hand him his pipe. Let us not appear before him to-morrow."

When the King awoke, neither of them was near. He called the lads to him and said: "I asked you once if you had anyone belonging to you, either father or mother; and you said you had no one. Why, then, are you so sad?"

And the brothers said: "Live long, O King! In truth, we have neither father nor mother. Even if we hide it from you we cannot hide it from God. We worked a little on a dwelling, but left the work unfinished and came away." And they told the King everything as it was.

---

[5] Southwest from the Sea of Wan lies a high mountain called Kraput-Koch ("Blue Ridge," from its blue color). Probably there was a dukedom or kingdom of Kraput-Koch which served as a city of refuge for the wandering Assyrian princes. Perhaps the legend has preserved in the person of the King of Kraput-Koch the memory of the Armenian prince Skajordi.

[6] Pipe-bearer.

[7] The servant who prepares the coffee.

The heart of the King was grieved, and he said: "My children, if such is the case, to-morrow I will give you some court servants. Go and finish your house."

Then the King arose and gave them forty servants, skilful workers, and each had a mule and a bridle.

Early in the morning they arose and loaded the beasts with their tools, and the two brothers led them to the dwelling. They travelled on and at last reached the spring and the threshold of their house.

Now Sanassar said to Abamelik: "Brother, shall we build the house first or the huts for the servants? These poor wretches cannot camp out in the sun."

And they began first to make the huts. So strong was Abamelik that he built ten huts every day, while the others brought in wood for their building. In four days they finished forty huts, and then they set about building the house and finished it. They set up stone pillars in rows—so powerful were they—and laid a stone base under them, and the house was made ready.

Abamelik rode to the King of Kraput-Koch and said: "We are thy children. We have built our castle: it is finished, and we come to you and entreat you, 'Come and give our dwelling a name,'" It pleased the King of Kraput-Koch that Abamelik had done this, and he said: "I rejoice that you have not forgotten me."

So the King gave Abamelik his daughter in marriage and made him his close friend. After the wedding the King and the young pair came together at the palace—and Uncle Toross [8] was with them—and they mounted their horses and departed. Abamelik rode before them to point out the way. When they were approaching the castle the King suddenly turned his horse as if to ride back again, and said: "You have given your castle a name and have purposely brought me here to try me."

Abamelik said: "May your life be long, O master! Believe me, we have given the castle no name. We have but built it and made it ready."

"Very well. It may be that you have given it no name,

---

[8] Probably the King's brother.

but as you have set up rows of stone pillars let us call it Sausun or Sassun." [9]

Here they remained several days. Uncle Toross was also married and stayed at Sassun, but the King returned home.

And Abamelik was strong and became a mighty man. From the environs of the Black Mountain and the Peak of Zetzinak, from Upper Musch as far as Sechanssar and the Plains of Tschapachtschur, [10] he reigned, and built a wall around his dominions. He made four gates. Often he shut his doors, mounted his horse, and captured whatever came in his way, both demons and beasts of prey. Once he penetrated into Mösr and ravaged it, and he went in to the wife of the Lord of Mösr and lay with her. She bore a son, and the King of Mösr knew that the boy was Abamelik's and named him Mösramelik. But afterward Abamelik slew the King and took his wife and became King of Mösr. [11]

*　　*　　*

Now Sanassar dwelt at Sassun, but the gods of his fathers gave him no repose, so he travelled to Bagdad to the home of his father and mother. His father, sitting at his window, saw his son Sanassar come riding up, and recognized him, and the caliph said: "My life to thee, great god! Thou hast brought back thy victim. Certainly in thy might thou wilt restore the second soon."

The mother—she was a Christian—began to weep and shed tears over her children. The father took a sharp sword and went out to meet his son, saying: "Come, my son, let us worship the great god in his temple. I must sacrifice to him."

---

[9] "Sassun" signifies "pillar upon pillar." This explains the origin of the name of Sassun, a district of the old Armenian province Achznik, south of the city of Musch. The residents of this district up to the present day owe their independence to their inaccessible dwelling-place.

[10] The names cited here exist to the present day. The places lie in the old districts of the Turuberan and Achznik in the present district Musch.

[11] The Armenians now call Egypt Mösr. This probably refers to Mossul.

The son said, "Dear father, your god is great and very wonderful. Truly in the night he permits us no rest. Certainly he will bring the second victim to you by force."

And they went into the temple of the god, and the son said: "Father dear, you know that we left your house when we were yet children, and we knew not the might of your god."

"Yes, yes, my son, but kneel before him and pray."

The son said: "What a wonderful god your god is! When you bowed before your god, there was a darkness before my eyes and I did not see how you did it. Bow once more before him, that I may learn to worship him."

When the father did the second time the son cried: "Bread and wine, the Lord liveth!" and seized his club and hurled the caliph full seven yards distant to the ground. And with his club he shattered all the images where they stood, put the silver in the skirts of his robe and carried it to his mother, saying: "Take this, mother, and wear it for ornament!"

His mother fell full length and bowed herself and said: "I thank thee, Creator of heaven and earth. It is well that thou hast rescued me from the hands of this cruel man."

They found Sanassar a wife and placed him on the throne in his father's place, and he remained at Bagdad. [12]

Now Abamelik, who reigned in Mösr, left his son Mösramelik to rule in his stead and went to Sassun. Many years passed and children were born to him. To one he gave the name Tschentschchapokrik. The eldest son he named Zöra-wegi, the second Zenow-Owan; while the third son was called Chor-Hussan, [13] and the youngest David.

Of these, Tschentschchapokrik and Zöranwegi proved to be ne'er-do-weels. Zenow-Owan had such a voice that he dried seven buffalo hides in the sun and wound them round his body so that it should not rend him. But the

---

[12] Here the story of Sanassar breaks off and he is not mentioned again in the tale.

[13] All these names are poetic and refer to certain characteristics of their bearers. "Zenow-Owan" means "melodiously-speaking John"; "Chor-Hussan" means "good singer"; "Tchentschchapokrik" means "sparrow"; and "Zöranwegi," "cowardly Wegi."

cleverest of all was David, and to his strength words cannot do justice.

Abamelik's life was long, but old age came upon him. Once he sat sunk in thought and said to himself: "Enemies are all about me. Who will care for my children after my death? Mösramelik alone can do this, for none beside him can cope with my enemies."

He set out to visit Mösramelik, [14] but he was very aged. "Mösramelik, my son," he said, "you are truly of my blood. If I die before you, I intrust my children to you. Take care of them. If you die first, confide yours to me and I will watch over them."

He returned and lived in his castle. His time came and he died. Then Mösramelik came and took the children to his house, for he had not forgotten his father's command. Sassun mourned the death of Abamelik for seven years. Then the peasants feasted and drank again with Uncle Toross, for they said: "Uncle Toross, our lads have grown old and our pretty girls are old women. If thou thinkest that by our seven years of weeping Abamelik will live again we would weep seven years longer." Uncle Toross gave the peasants their way, and said: "Marry your lads and maidens. Weeping leads nowhere."

And they sat down and feasted and drank wine. Uncle Toross took a cup in his hand and paused: he was thinking about something, and he neither drank nor set the cup down. His son cries from the street: "Father, dear, there are the mad men of Sassun. Take care, they will be jeering at you. Let us go away."

Uncle Toross turned to his son and said: "Oh, you dog of a son! Shall I sit here and feast? Did not Mösramelik come and take our children away? Abamelik's children in trouble, and I sitting at a banquet? Oh, what a shame it is! Bread and wine, God be praised! Truly, I will drink no wine till I have fetched the little ones." And Uncle Toross went out of Sassun and came to Mösr. He greeted Mösramelik, and they sat down together. Said Uncle Toross: "Now, we are come for God's judgment. It is true that you made an agreement with

---

[14] To Mossul.

Abamelik, but if a man sells a captive he should first wait on the lord." [15]

They arose and went to the court, [16] and Uncle Toross was given the children.

But Mösramelik stood in fear of these children, and he said to Uncle Toross, "Let these children first pass under my sword, and then take them with you."

Uncle Toross told the lads of this, and Zöranwegi said, "Let us pass under his sword and escape hence"; and the other two said the same. But David said otherwise: "If he wishes us dead he will not kill us to-day, for the people will say he has murdered the children. Under his sword I will not go. He does this so that I shall not lift my sword against him when I am a man." Uncle Toross got the boys together, that they might pass under the sword of Mösramelik, for he was very anxious. David was rebellious; he stood still and went not under it. Uncle Toross seized his collar and pushed him, but David would not go. He ran past it at one side and kicked with his great toe upon a flint until the sparks flew. And Mösramelik was frightened and said: "This child is still so young and yet is terrible. What will happen when he is a man! If any evil comes to me it will be through him."

Uncle Toross took the children and came to Sassun. Zöranwegi he established in the castle in his father's place, but David, who was the youngest, was sent out to herd the calves.

What a boy David was! If he struck out at the calves with his oaken stick, he would throw them all down, and forty others beside. Once he drove the calves to the top of the mountain. He found a herdsman there who was abusing his calves, and said: "You fellow! What are you up to? Wait now, if I catch you, you will get something from my oaken stick that will make you cry Ow! ow!"

The fellow answered David: "I am ready to give my life for your head if I am not a shepherd from your father's village. These calves, here, belong to the peasants."

---

[15] This means that if a captive is to be sold his kinsmen have a right before all others to redeem him.

[16] Schariat, the name of the Turkish court of justice, stands in the original.

David said, "If that is so, watch my calves also. I know not what time I should drive them home. When the time comes tell me, that I may drive them in."

Then David drove in the calves on time that day, and Uncle Toross was pleased and said: "Always be punctual, my son; go out and come back every day at the right time."

"Uncle Toross, it was not my wisdom that did this. I have hired a comrade who will watch over my calves and see that I am ready with them."

Once his comrade tarried, and David was greatly vexed. It appeared that a religious festival was held in the village, and on this account the young man was detained. Finally he arrived, and David said to him, "To-day you get nothing from me."

The young man said: "David, I am willing to die for you. From fear of your anger, I waited not for the end of the service of God in the church, and not one spoonful of the holy soup [17] has passed my lips. I drove out the calves and am here. Now you know why I tarried."

David said: "Wait here; I will bring you your dinner." He set off with his oaken stick over his shoulder. He came to the village, and found that all the people had brought corn to the priests, who blessed it. David stuck his oaken stick through the handle of the four-handled kettle, and, full as it was, lifted it to his shoulder and walked away. The priests and the peasants wondered at it, and one cried, "Truly, he has carried off a kettle!"

A priest cried out, "For God's sake, be silent! It is one of those mad men of Sassun. Take care or he will come back and break our ribs for us. May he take the thing and fall down with it!"

And David took the kettle of grits to his comrade, whom he found weeping on the mountain.

"Ha, ha," said David, "I know why you weep. I have

---

[17] Although the Armenians became Christians in the fourth century, they still retain many heathen customs which have lost all their original significance. They still sacrifice sheep and cows which have on the previous evening been given some salt consecrated by the priests. The meat is cooked in immense kettles and carried around to the houses. The shepherd speaks of soup of this kind.

brought the grits, but have forgotten butter and salt. That is why you weep. Eat the grits now, and have salt and butter this evening."

But the youth said. "David, I am ready to die for you, What need have I of salt and butter; forty thieving Dews have come and driven away our calves."

David said, "Stay here and watch these calves, and I will bring back all the others"; and he went after the calves. He followed their tracks to the entrance of a cave and paused. He cried out with so loud a voice that the Dews were frightened, and were as full of fear as is the devil when Christ's voice is heard in hell.

And when the leader of the Dews heard the voice he said: "That is surely David, Abamelik's son. Go receive him with honor, else he will strike us dead."

They went out, one by one, and David struck each as he passed with his oaken cudgel, so that their heads fell off and only dead bodies remained in the place. He cut off the ears of all the forty and buried them under a stone at the mouth of the cave.

He laid down his club and entered the cave. There he saw a heap of gold and a heap of silver—indeed, all the treasures of the world. Since his father's death they had robbed and concealed their plunder in this cavern. He opened a door, and saw a steed standing fastened to a ring. David was sunk in thought, and said to himself: "Uncle dear, this property belongs to you, but this beast to me. If you give it to me—good. If not, you travel after those other fellows." Then he answered for Uncle Toross: "My child, the treasure and the beast should belong to you. What shall I do with them?"

He looked around and saw upon a pyre a copper kettle with four handles, and in it were his forty calves. He stuck his oaken stick through the handles and raised the kettle, poured off the water, pushed the calves' feet back into the kettle, lifted it to his shoulder, and went back to his comrade.

The two drove the rest of the herd into the village, and David called the owners to him and said: "If you deceive my brother a hair's breadth in the reckoning it will go badly with you. Sell this kettle. May it repay you for your calves."

69

He separated his own calves from the peasants, and went home. It was then midday. He said to Uncle Toross: "Take quickly twenty asses and we will go out and bring back treasure that shall suffice you and your children till the seventh generation."

And they took the asses and set forth. When they reached the cavern, Uncle Toross saw the bodies of the Dews stretched near the entrance, and they were swelled up like hills. In great fright Uncle Toross loosed his ass from the others and fell back.

David said: "You destroyer! I fled not before them living, but you fear them dead! If you believe me not, turn back and raise this stone. I concealed all their ears there."

Uncle Toross came back and took the asses, and they went into the cave. They made a pack of all the treasure and carried it away with them. David said: "All this treasure belongs to you, but the steed is mine. If you will not give it to me, you shall follow after them."

He answered: "My child, the horse and the treasure too are yours. What should I do with it?"

Uncle Toross let David mount the steed. He gave him the spurs and he bucked to right and left. This was no ordinary steed—the difficulties of managing him cannot be described.

They returned to Sassun with the treasure. David procured a beautiful falcon and rode off to hunt. The calves he had long ago given over.

Once, as he hunted, he rode across the soil of a poor man, whose family numbered seven heads, and the man had seven beds of millet. Four beds he laid waste, and three remained. Someone ran with the news to the old graybeard and said: "You are ruined. Go at once to your field, for before night he will destroy the other three beds."

The graybeard rose early and went out and saw his field was laid waste. He glanced about and saw David coming with a falcon on his hand. The graybeard cursed David and said: "Dost thou not fear God? Dost thou test thy strength on my grain-field? I have seven mouths to fill, and seven millet beds. Four thou hast destroyed, and three remain! If you are brave, go and get back your inheritance that extends from the summit of Mount Zözmak as far as

Sechanssar. Mösramelik has taken it from you and draws wealth from it Go and get it back. Why try your strength on me?"

But David answered: "Old man, curse me not. Here is a handful of gold—use it." And as he said it he killed his falcon.

David returned home and said: "Uncle Toross, go and bring me my father's staff and bow. I am going to make war, for others consume my inheritance and none of you have said anything about it to me."

Uncle Toross arose and demanded of Zöranwegi in David's name the staff and bow of Abamelik, but Zöranwegi refused it. David sent a second time, saying: "If you give it to me, good. If not, I will see to it that your head flies off and only your body remains."

Zöranwegi was frightened, and surrendered the bow and baton, and Uncle Toross brought them to David. And David fell asleep and dreamed. The next day he took forty calves and went to holy Maratuk, [18] where he slaughtered the forty calves and bathed in their blood. Then he fell on his face and prayed and wept until God sent from heaven a sacred sign and a token. Even now the holy sign is to be found in Hawar at the house of Sork. David kissed the holy sign and put it under the right shoulder, and the token under the left.

Mösramelik knew that David, Abamelik's son, was come into manhood, and he gathered together a host to march against him. And he appointed a *holbaschi,* [19] who prepared his army and attacked David at Maratuk. He met on the march seven women, and said to them, "Sing and dance until I return," and they answered: "Why shall we dance and sing? We know not what we should say."

And Holbaschi sang for them:

"May the little women busy themselves grinding corn; May the stout women help with the camel-loading; For Holbaschi carries grim war to Sassun. Strong yoke-oxen and red milch-cows he'll bring back In the springtime; butter and Tochorton Will be plentiful in the Land of Mösr."

---

[18] Maratuk is a monastery built on a mountain of the same name.
[19] This Turkish title shows that the legend has been altered at a late date.

Holbaschi saw the women begin dancing and singing, and started his host again and went to Maratuk and entered its gates. The daughter of the priest of Maratuk had often glanced slyly at David, and he was not indifferent to her. The priest's daughter went to David and said: "David, I am ready to die for you! Arise and see how many warriors are congregated in the courtyard."

When she had spoken she went out and closed all the gates from without. David stretched himself and cried: "Bread and wine, the Lord liveth!" and began to knock off the heads of the men of war. He beheaded them so that the bodies flew over the walls and the heads remained lying in the court. And he laid hold of Holbaschi, and tore out his teeth and drove them into his brow like nails. And he bent his lance till it curved like a dog's collar and put it around his neck. "Now," he said, "take yourself off and tell all to Mösramelik. If people still remain in his country let him herd them together before I come."

Holbaschi met the women a second time, and they were singing and dancing. And one of them sang:

"Holbaschi, dear Holbaschi, went hence like a cruel wolf. Why come you back to us like a hunting dog? Your lance lies on your neck like a dog's collar, Thy mouth gapes like an open window, And slime flows out like curdled milk from a skin; [20] And whole caravans of flies buzz round it."

And Holbaschi sang:

"Oh, you shameless, worthless hussies, I thought that Sassun was a free field. Think not that only rocks and clefts opposed me. There new-born children are fierce devils, Their arrows like beams of the oil-mill; And like windows they tear out the mouths of their enemies. All the brave lads who went with me Arefallenin Charaman. [21] In the spring its waters will bring you booty, Then your butter and cheese can be made."

Now David armed himself and marched against

---

[20] In Armenia, as is usual in the East, they make butter out of curdled milk; and for this reason the vessel is always covered with scum.
[21] A valley near Musch.

Mösramelik. He found a great host assembled and encamped near Sechanssar. [22]

David said: "I promise thee not to give battle till I have eaten rice pillau in the green and red tent," and he urged his horse forward and appeared suddenly from the west in front of the tent. Great fright possessed the army when they perceived this rider, and Melik said, "What manner of man art thou?"

"I am the son of a western king, and I have come to help you."

Melik pitched a tent for him, and they ate together seven days. On the eighth day David mounted his horse, rode twice before Mösramelik's tent, and said: "Now, come out, I want to fight you. How long, Mösramelik, are you going to encroach upon my inheritance?" And David cried: "Bread and wine, God lives!" and fighting began on all sides.

Uncle Toross heard of the combat. He tore up a poplar by its roots, threw it across his shoulder, and set out. He halted at the upper end of the valley in which the fight was going on. If anyone crept away David shouted: "Dear Uncle Toross, chase him back into the valley and I will be ready for him!"

At last the army began to murmur: "Let them struggle hand to hand. He who overpowers the other has conquered."

Then said one of them. "Sit down, that I may slay you with my club," and the other said: "No, you sit down." At last they agreed that David, being the youngest, should sit, So he put his shield over his head, laid under it the holy cross, and sat down. Mösramelik made an onset from three leagues, burst upon him, and assailed him with a club, saying, "Earth thou art, be earth again!"

David said: "I believe in the high and holy cross of Maratuk. It is to me as if I were still eating rice pillau under the red and green tent."

Mösramelik sprung upon him three times, struck him with his club, and said: "Earth thou art, be earth again!" and David replied only, "I believe in the high and holy cross of Maratuk."

Then came Mösramelik's turn to sit down, and he was

---

[22] Literally, a table-like mountain.

stubborn and would not. But the army reproached him and put his shield over his head, and he sat down. Then came Mösramelik's mother, and began to ask mercy, saying: "David, I am ready to die for you! Is he not thy brother? Slay him not; have pity on him!"

"O shameless woman! When he struck me, thou saidst not, 'Is he not thy brother!' But, may your wish be granted! One blow I will give up for God's sake, the second for your sake, but the third belongs to me, and when I strike either he dies or lives!"

David rode back and forward again, and seizing his club hurled Mösramelik seven yards deep into the earth. Then he ravaged Mösr and ascended the throne.

*   *   *

The Emir [23] of Kachiswan had a daughter, and her name was Chandud-Chanum. [24] Chandud-Chanum heard of David's valor, and gave gifts to a bard and said to him: "Go, sing to David of my beauty, that he may come hither and we may love each other."

The bard went to Sassun, for he thought David was there. He came to Sassun and entered Zöranwegi's castle, thinking David lived in it, and sat down and began to sing to Zöranwegi. Zöranwegi cried: "Go. Club him and hunt him forth. He thinks to bring David hither by cunning!"

They set upon the singer, dragged him to the valley, and threw him into the road. In the evening the shepherds returned on their oxen to the village. An ox became wild, and the herdsman fell off, and seeking the cause he found the bard, who wept and lamented and asked the herdsman:

"Which of the brothers lives in that castle?"

The shepherd answered: "Here lives Zöranwegi; yonder, in Mösr, David."

And the bard gave a piece of gold to the shepherds, and they gathered up the pieces of his broken tambur [25] and pointed out his way to him. He went and sang of Chandud-

---

[23] "Emir," in the eyes of the orientals, is almost the same as "king."

[24] "Chandud" is a woman's name. "Chanum" means "lady."

[25] An instrument like a guitar.

Chanum's beauty before David. David rewarded him richly, and said, "Go before, I will come," and the singer went and told all to Chandud-Chanum. [26]

David departed straightway and went by way of Sassun and the Heights of Zözmak. He found a plough [27] standing in his way. He freed the oxen, seized the plough-chain, mounted his horse, and dragged the plough down. And it fell from the summit of the Black Mountain plump into the aqueduct of the village of Marnik.

He drew on and perceived that a buffalo had got loose and run along the road and left its dung there. David looked at the dung and said: "If evil befalls me he is guilty of it who left the dung there; if not, it is also his work that it befalls me not."

From a side-path appeared a buffalo, and David had never seen the like before. He lifted his club to slay him when from the opposite side a shepherd came and began to scold the buffalo. David thought the shepherd was scolding him and said, "Fellow, what have I done to you that you rail at me?"

The shepherd answered: "Who are you? Ah, you are a Sassun brawler who has seen nothing of the world! I spoke to my buffalo."

"Don't be angry, youngster! It is a shame, indeed, that in my country I have never seen the like. Are there many such creatures in these parts?"

The shepherd said, "Come, and I will show you."

And they went to the field of August, where the peasants hitched their buffaloes and drove them. David found the buffaloes with tongues lolling from the heat as they drew the plough. David felt pity for them; he unhitched them and drove them to the pond.

The ploughman began to curse him, and he said: "Ploughman, curse me not; only give me the chain into my hand."

---

[26] The song in which the bard praises the beauty of Chandud-Chanum is wanting. A certain carelessness is seen generally in the rest of the narrative.

[27] The Armenians use, in ploughing, a kind of plough which is drawn by from five to ten pairs of buffaloes or oxen.

75

He seized the chain and began to draw; the ploughman guided the plough and David ploughed nine furrows. Then the shepherd said to David: "That is not thy strength. Leave thy horse and then draw. We shall see whether it is thine or thy horse's strength."

David left his horse and ploughed nine furrows alone.

The shepherd then said to David: "It is already noon. Come now and eat, then thou canst go on thy way!"

David answered: "No, I will ride on. Thy children want to eat, and if I come nothing will remain for them."

However, they sat down and when the dinner was set out David crumbled all the bread and the vessels all at once, and the shepherd said: "Here, hide yourselves or he will devour us also."

David said: "Surely, brother, he who drags the plough must eat bread. How could it be otherwise?"

And he went his way to the city where Chandud-Chanum dwelt.

*   *   *

David came to the gates of the castle where Chandud-Chanum lived—to the place where all her suitors came to woo. He saw a youth standing near the door with a club in his hand, David said: "Ha, my lad, what do they call you?"

"My name is Gorgis."

"Gorgis!" said David. "When I marry Chandud-Chanum you shall be godfather! Now, Godfather Gorgis, who is in the house?"

"Matchmakers from the giants—Schibikan of Chorassan and Hamsa of Lori."

David said, "Take my horse and fasten him." And he took his horse and tied him.

Then David asked: "What kind of a club have you? Show it me."

David took the club and threw it into the air with such force that it is whirring till this very day. Then he said, "Godfather Gorgis, let us go in and eat and drink."

They went in, and David sat down, for he was tired and hungry, and every matchmaker, one after the other, handed David a cup of wine. David lost patience and seized the wine-pitcher and emptied it in one draught, saying, "Now say only what is well for you!"

The wine made David drunk, and when he let his head fall the matchmakers drew their swords to strike him, but when he raised his head they concealed their swords. They began this again when Godfather Gorgis called out: "Think not that you are in Georgia! No, this is a dangerous country." And when David heard him he said, "Now stand bravely at the door!"

The matchmakers sprang up and as they ran each gave Gorgis a box on the ear and escaped. David then turned to Gorgis and said: "Where can I see Chandud-Chanum?"

"In the garden of the King," Gorgis answered. "To-day is Friday and she will be there. Before her walk twenty slaves, and twenty walk behind her. We will go to-day and see her there."

So Gorgis and David went thither and concealed themselves behind the garden wall and waited. The slaves passed by one after another, and, when Chandud-Chanum came, David put his arm around her neck and kissed her three times. Chandud-Chanum said not a word. He kissed her again. Chandud-Chanum seized him by the collar and threw him against the wall so that the blood gushed from his nose.

David was angry and was going to mount his horse. "Godfather Gorgis," he said, "lead out my horse. I will destroy the city and depart."

Gorgis began to plead: "I pray you, put it off till morning. It is dark now. At daybreak arise and destroy the city and depart."

David lay in bed and could not sleep from anger. "Would it were dawn that I might rise and destroy the city and get away from here," he thought to himself.

Chandud-Chanum was still walking in the garden. A lame slave came to her and said: "Thy walk will end sadly. Take care, David is going to destroy the city and depart."

She took the cloth in which her evening meal had been brought, and wrapped her head in it. She turned and went straightway into the castle where David was and knocked at his door.

David said: "What insolent people live here! They will

77

not wait till morning, but say, 'Arise, destroy the city and be off!'"

Gorgis arose and looked out of the window and said, "These are women, not men," and they opened the door.

Chandud-Chanum came to David and said: "You kissed me first for the fatigue of your journey, a second time for yourself, and a third time for God's sake. Why did you kiss me a fourth time? You are the son of your father and I am the daughter of mine. It has been said: Take to yourself a wife that you may have a son who is like his uncle. Do you think you have brought me the heads of the giants Hamsa of Lori and Schibikan of Chorassan, that you kiss me a fourth time?"

David's heart softened and he said: "If that is so I will go out at daybreak and bring you their heads." Then he added: "Very well, I go; if they are stronger than I they will kill me. For God's sake come and seek my body. On the right hand I have a birth-mark—a cross—by that you shall know me. Bring my body back and bury it."

So David set out. The giants perceived a rider coming, for the dust from his horse's hoofs rose to heaven: "This rider comes to fight with us. Perhaps he is of the race of Sergo." [28]

They called to him, saying: "Ho, fellow! who are you, and whence come you? Do you know Chandud-Chanum? Will you take this ring to her?"

David said: "Certainly I know her, but I have come to take your heads to the Princess Chandud. I know nothing about your rings!"

The eyebrows of Schibikan of Chorassan hung down over his breast and he fastened them across his back. Hamsa of Lori had an underlip so long that it reached the ground and swept it.

David and the giants began to hack and hew each other and they fought with clubs and bows until night. David cried: "I believe in the high and holy cross of Maratuk," and took his sword and cut both their heads off. He bound

---

[28] Sergo-Sarkus (Sergius) so the Kurds called the Christians, regarding them as descendants of St. Sergius, who is very popular among the Armenians of Wan and Musch.

78

their hair together and hung them across his horse like saddle bags and their tongues furrowed the ground like a plough.

David rode away with their heads and had already traversed half the way when he saw approaching him, riding between heaven and earth, a rider, who called out to him! "Do you think you have conquered the giants Schibikan and Hamsa?" The rider sprang behind David and struck at him with a club. He crawled under the saddle and the club struck the stirrup and tore it loose, and it fell to the ground. David sprang out from under the saddle and cried: "Bread and wine, as the Lord liveth!" and swung his club over his enemy. The enemy dodged the blow, but his hair fell away from his face. David looked and recognized Chandud-Chanum; she had disguised herself and had come to meet him.

"O shameless woman!" David said. "You would disgrace me a second time."

They rode together into Chandud-Chanum's city. They arrived and dismounted and called Chandud Chanum's father. David said to him: "Will you give me your daughter for a wife?"

Her father said: "I will not give her to you. If you will marry her and live here, I will give her to you. If you must take her away, I will not give her. How can I do otherwise? I have enemies all around me; they will destroy my city."

And David said: "I will marry her and stay here. I will not take her away."

So they were married and celebrated the wedding, feasting seven days and seven nights.

The time passed by unheeded, and when nine months, nine days and nine hours had passed, God sent them a son.

And David said to Chandud-Chanum: "If this child is mine, he must have a mark—he will show great strength." They put the child in swaddling-clothes, but instead of bands they bound him with plough-chains. He began to cry and stir in his cradle and the chain snapped into pieces.

They sent word to David: "The youngster is a stout fellow. He has broken the chains. But one of his hands seems hurt. He clenches his fist, and no one can open it."

David came and sat down, looked at the hand and

79

opened it. In the hand he found a little lump of clotted blood. "The whole world is to him as a drop of blood, and he will hold it in his hand. If he lives he will do wonderful deeds."

Then they christened the boy and gave him the name of Mcher.

Time passed and the boy grew fast, and David left him in Kachiswan with his grandparents, and took Chandud-Chanum with him to Sassun. The men of Chlat [29] heard David's coming and they assembled an army, built a rampart, formed their wagons into a fortress, and began to give battle. When Chandud-Chanum sent her lance against the wall she shattered it and the wagons flew seven leagues away. Then David went forward and drove the fighters away, saying to them: "Ye men of Chlat! what shameless people ye be! Ye wage war on women! Let me but take my wife to Sassun and I will come back, and we will fight it out."

But the men of Chlat believed him not. "Swear to us by the holy cross you carry; then we will believe you," said they.

David touched the token with his hand as he thought, but the cross was there and he knew it not, and the power of the cross was that no one could swear by it.

He took Chandud-Chanum to Sassun. Here he first knew that he had sworn on the cross, for he found the cross lying at his left shoulder where the token had been.

"Now it will go badly with me," said David. "Whether I go or whether I stay, it will go badly with me. And I must go."

He advanced, therefore, to give battle, and the men of Chlat pressed him sorely. His horse was caught in the reedy marsh of Tschechur. [30] With difficulty he crawled out of the bog and reached the waters of the Lochur. [31]

Once Abamelik had lingered at the house of Ibraham Aga, and forcibly entered the sleeping-room of his wife. Her

---

[29] The city of Chlat (Turkish "Achlat") lies northwest of the Sea of Wan. In olden times it was famous for its splendor, its high walls, and its citadel. The inhabitants had been injured by David's father and wished to avenge themselves.

[30] A marsh at the outlet of the Kara-Su, a tributary of the Euphrates.

[31] A small river which empties into the Sea of Wan not far from Chlat.

name was Schemschen-Chanum. She had borne a daughter to Abamelik, who was now an ardent Mahometan. This daughter took up her bow and arrows and concealed herself on the sloping river-bank. When David bathed in the waters of Locher she shot him, assassin-like, with an arrow in the back. David arose and made a great outcry and his voice sounded even up to Sassun. Zönow-Owan, Chorassan, Uncle Toross, Tschöntschchapokrik, and Zöranwegi came together, for they heard the voice of David. And Zönow-Owan called to him from Sassun, "We are coming."

And they went forth to help David, who heard in the water the voice of his kinsmen. They came to the river and found David, who said: "Zönow-Owan, she seemed frightened at our calling. Go and find her."

And they sought and found the blue-eyed maiden. David seized her by one foot, trod on the other, tore her in pieces, and threw her into the village at the foot of the mountain. From this deed he named the village Tschiwtis-Tschapkis. [32] The village lies at the mouth of the Tschechur and is called Tschapkis to this day.

The brothers took David with them and moved on to Sassun. And after four days David died, and his brothers mourned for him. They went to Chandud-Chanum to console her and wish her long life; but Chandud-Chanum said, "Ah, me, after David's death I am but the subject of your scorn."

And Tschöntschchapokrik said: "Chandud-Chanum, weep not, weep not. David is dead, but my head is still whole."

Chandud-Chanum climbed the tower and threw herself down. Her head struck a stone and made a hole in it, and into this hole the men of Sassun pour millet and grind as the people of Mösr do; and every traveller from Mösr stops there before the castle to see the stone.

The brothers came to see the body of Chandud-Chanum, and they pressed on her breasts and milk flowed therefrom. They said: "Surely she has a child! If there is a child it must be in Kachiswan." [33] And they set out for

---

[32] Literally, "I will tear in pieces and scatter."
[33] The small city of Kagisman, not far from Kars.

Kachiswan and said to the governor: "A child of our brother and sister-in-law lives here. Where is it?"

"It is not here."

"We have a sign. In the breast of our sister-in-law was milk."

Then the governor said: "She had a daughter, but it is dead."

"We have a test for that also—for our dead. The grave of one dead one year is one step long, of one dead two years, two steps long, and so on."

They went to the church-yard and found not a single grave which stood their test.

Zönow-Owan said: "Bind leather bands about me. I will cry out."

The truth was, they had dug a cellar for Mcher underground, and hid him there and watched over him.

The brothers bound Zönow-Owan about the body and he cried out. Mcher knew his voice and would have gone to him, but his grandmother said to him: "That is not the voice of thy kinsman. It is the noise of children and the beating of drums."

When Mcher heard the voice for the third time he beat down the door and went out. One door destroyed the other. By a blow of his fist he sent the first door against the second, the second against the third, and so all seven doors were shattered.

Mcher saw his uncles from afar, but his father was not there. He asked, and his uncle told him the men of Chlat had slain his father. He fell upon his face and wept, and as he lay there his uncles wished to lift him, but exert themselves as they would they could not move him.

The tears of Mcher furrowed the earth and flowed like a river. After three days he arose, mounted his father's horse, and rode to Chlat. He circled the town and destroyed it—as it is even to this day. Then he ascended the mountain Memrut 34 and saw the smoke of the ruins grow ever denser. Only one old woman remained alive. He seized her, and,

---

34 A high mountain not far from Chlat northwest of the Sea of Wan. Many interesting legends about it exist. Haik, the ancestor of the Armenian Nimrod, is said to be buried here.

bending two trees down, bound her feet to the trees and let them loose. And thus he killed her. Since then no smoke ascends from Chlat.

Mcher permitted his uncles to return to their own dwelling-places and himself rode toward Tosp.

Men say he is still there, and they show his house, and even now water flows from the rocks for his horse.

On Ascension-night the door of Mcher's rock opens. But it is decreed that he shall not go out: the floor holds him not, his feet sink into the earth.

Once on Ascension-night a shepherd saw Mcher's door open, and the shepherd entered. Mcher asked him: "By what occupation do you live?"

"By brains," said the shepherd.

Then Mcher said: "We shall see what kind of brains you have! Take the nose-bag of my horse and hang it around his neck."

The shepherd tried with all his might, but could not lift the bag. He led the horse to the bag, opened it, and put the straps around the horse's neck. The horse raised his head and lifted the bag. The shepherd led him back to his place and said, "That is the sort of brains by which we live in the world."

Then the shepherd said, "Mcher, when will you leave this place?"

Mcher answered: "When plum-trees bear wheat and wild-rose bushes barley, it is appointed I shall leave this place."

And three apples fell down from heaven—one for the story-teller, one for the hearer, and the other for the whole world.

*　　*　　*

THE RUINED FAMILY
BY
GABRIEL SUNDUKIANZ
[Translated by F.B. Collins, B.S.]

DRAMATIS PERSONAE

OSSEP GULABIANZ, a merchant.
SALOME, his wife.
NATO, his daughter.
CHACHO, Ossep's aunt.
GEWO, a merchant, Ossep's friend.
ALEXANDER MARMAROW, a young official.
BARSSEGH LEPROINK, a merchant.
KHALI, his wife.
MOSI, Leproink's relative.
MICHO, shop-boy at Leproink's.
DARTSCHO, clerk at Leproink's.
MARTHA, Salome's friend.

Guests, an executor, his secretary, creditors, witnesses, and several servants.
The scene is Tiflis. The first and third acts take place in Ossep's house, the second in Barssegh's.

THE RUINED FAMILY
ACT I

Well-furnished room with open door in centre and ante-room behind. To the left in foreground a window looking out upon a garden. To the right a sofa, in front of which is a table. To the left a tachta [35] with a ketscha [36] and several mutakas. [37] A side door.

---

[35] Broad, low sofa.
[36] Carpet.
[37] Long, round pillows.

Scene I

Salome. Chacho.

SALOME [*from back of stage*]. You're welcome. Come, come, I beg of you. Dear aunt, how can I thank you for taking the trouble to come here!

CHACHO [*covered by a tschadra* [38] *enters from the right of the ante-chamber*]. Good-morning! [*Taking off the tschadra.*] Why did you send for me in such haste? [*Gives one end of the tschadra to Salome*].

SALOME [*taking hold of one end of the tschadra*]. Dear aunt, I am in such a desperate mood that if someone were to pierce my heart not a drop of blood would flow. [*While she is speaking they fold the tschadra*].

CHACHO. So it seems that it cannot be managed?

SALOME. How could it be managed, dear aunt? They insist upon having 8,000 rubles. Ossep will not give so much. You know what a miser he is!

CHACHO. Yes, he is really odd.

SALOME. But, dear aunt, God would surely not allow an affair like this to come to nothing for the sake of 2,000 rubles. What, am I to let a man of such social position and such brilliancy escape me?

CHACHO. Great heaven, how can anyone be so obstinate!

SALOME. That is just why I begged you to come to us. Speak to Ossep about it, and perhaps your words will soften him.

CHACHO. I will talk with him; yes, indeed, I will talk to him. We cannot neglect a matter of such importance, my child. [*Lays the tschadra under the tachta covering the ketscha*

---

[38] A long veil, covering the head and upper part of the body.

and sits down on it.] Great heaven, how sore the pavement has made my feet!

SALOME [*seating herself on a chair*]. May God reward you, dear aunt! May the Holy Mother be a protectress for your children as you are now for my Nato.

CHACHO. Is not Nato my child also? Is she a stranger to me? I am altogether charmed with her beautiful form. But where is the child? Is she not at home?

SALOME. Yes, certainly; she is dressing. You understand, dear aunt, how you are to talk to him? Perhaps you will succeed with him. They expect the final answer to-day; this morning the young man's sister was here, and she may be here again any minute.

CHACHO. Don't be afraid, dear child. Calm yourself. Where is Ossep? What does he think about it?

SALOME. He is busy, but he will be here directly. He says, and insists upon it, that he will allow our daughter to marry no one but a business man.

CHACHO. He is right, my child; a good business man is worth much. Yes; is not one who has money in his pockets the best?

SALOME. Oh, how you talk! What business man is to be compared with Alexander Marmarow! Is there any business man worthy to untie his shoe-strings? His politeness alone is worth more than ten business men. Lately he honored us with a visit, and I was so fascinated with his manners! and beside he is still young; is handsome; is educated; has a good position and a good salary and will advance every day— everybody says so. Perhaps some day he will be governor.

CHACHO. That is all very well, dear Salome; but if the thing cannot be done, what then? One must submit, to some extent, to the head of the family. A good business man never suffers from hunger, and lives without wanting anything. I don't know what has gotten into your heads. Officials! always officials!

SALOME. You speak well, dear aunt, but Nato would not marry a business man at any price. I would thank God if she would. Would I be so stupid as not to be glad of it? The deuce take these times! This comes of too much study: the girls now mind neither father nor mother!

CHACHO. Yes; how the world has changed! The streams and the hills are the same, but the people are different! But, by the way, Salome, do you know what I have heard? They say that Leproink is trying for him also; is that true?

SALOME. Yes, yes, dear aunt, a lot of go-betweens go to his house. But God will surely not let a man like that become his son-in-law while my daughter is left to become the wife of a shopkeeper.

CHACHO. Who would have believed that this Barssegh would have worked himself up like that! Yet God be praised! Perhaps it is the times that bring it about. Yesterday or the day before he was a shop-boy at Basaschoma, [39] and now! I can picture him as he was then! He wore a *tschocha* [40] of green camelot with a narrow purple belt. The wadding stuck out at his elbows and his boots were mended in four places. Great piles of goods were loaded on the poor devil's shoulders. Many a time, with the yardstick in one hand, he came to our houses with whole pieces of calico and got a few pennies from us for his trouble. And now he is a man of some importance! Many's the time we gave him a cuff and sent him back and forth with his goods. And, Salome, do you know that he lied? God save us from such lies! But what could he do? One would die of hunger, to be sure, if one always told the truth.

SALOME. Yes, yes, dear aunt, it is the same Barssegh— whom they all call "Wassil Matwejitsch" now.

---

[39] A bazaar in Tiflis.

[40] A long overcoat.

CHACHO. What! have they turned Mathus, his father, into Matjewitsch? Who is good enough for them now? Many a time has the cobbler, Mathus, mended my shoes. His workshop was in the Norasch quarter. O good heavens, the world is upside down!

Scene II

NATO [*entering at right*]. Mamma! O aunt, are you here, too?
[*Hugs her and kisses her*].

CHACHO. O my only treasure! [*Kisses her.*] How fresh and pretty you are! Where are you going? Are you going out when I have just come?

NATO. What are you saying, dear aunt? I will come back again immediately. I am only going to make a few purchases at the bazaar. [*Turning to Salome*] Dear mamma——
[*They begin to speak together in a low tone*].

CHACHO [*aside*]. Yes, yes, her father is right! [*Aloud.*] I will go and see what the children are doing [*trying to rise*]. Come here, you pretty rogue, and give me your hand. I feel exhausted.
[*Nato helps her*].

SALOME [*offering her hand*]. Let me help you, too.

CHACHO. May God give you health and a life as long as mine! [*To Nato:*] O my heart's angel—if only I have my wish and see you wear the bridal wreath!

SALOME. God grant it, dear aunt!

CHACHO. He will, he will, my child! [*Going toward the entrance.*] Good heaven! how old I have grown!
[*Goes out at the left*].

NATO. Don't keep me waiting, mamma.

SALOME. And won't a little less satisfy you? Why do you want so much all of a sudden?

NATO. But, dear mamma, please; I want it so much!

SALOME [*putting her hand in her pocket*]. I can never get away from you.
[*Takes out her purse and looks for something in it*].

NATO [*holding out her hand*]. You have it there, mamma.

SALOME. Have a little patience. [*Takes out some money and gives it to her.*] Take it! take it! though I know your father will scold about it.

NATO. But what can I do, when I need it so badly?

SALOME. Need it—nonsense! There is no end of your needs. [*Pulling at Nato's hat.*] How have you put your hat on again? And the flowers are all pulled apart.
[*Arranges it*].

NATO. Bah! what difference does that make?

SALOME. You're crazy! [*Removes her veil.*] How have you put on your veil? I must ever and eternally fix something on you!

NATO. You will make me too beautiful, mamma.

SALOME. Whether I make you beautiful or not, it will make no difference. You will be only the wife of a merchant.

NATO. Yes, yes, I have been expecting that!

SALOME. And you really think that your father will ask you?

NATO. And whom should he ask?

SALOME. Think what you will; he will not let his decision be altered by you. He says, "I will give her only to a business man."

NATO. Yes, yes, surely.

SALOME. By heaven!

NATO. Mamma, is what you say true?

SALOME. As true as the sun shines above you. He spoke of it again to-day.

NATO. It is decided, then?

SALOME. What am I to do if there is no other way out? You know we have not any too much money.

NATO. And you are going to make a shopkeeper's wife of me, so that everyone will laugh at me [*ready to cry*]; so that I shall be an object of scorn for all. And why have you had me so well educated? Have I learned Russian and French and piano-playing for a man of that sort? What does a shopkeeper want of a piano? Pickle-jars and butter-tubs are useful to him, but not my French! I am curious as to how he would speak to me: *Moi aller, vous joli tu voir*.

SALOME. Enough! enough! you wild girl!

NATO [*crying*]. It is out of the question, mamma. No, not for the world could I marry a business man! I will not have one! I would rather jump into the water than marry one! [*Crying, she gives the money back.*] Take it back! What do I need it for now? Why should I go out and make purchases? For whom, then?
[*Takes off her mantle, flings her parasol aside, sits down on the sofa and begins to cry*].

90

SALOME. O great heaven! is this not torture? I get it on both sides. [*Turning to Nato*:] Be still, you stupid girl!

NATO. For this I have learned so much; for this you have brought me up so grandly and given yourself so much trouble and care! [*Weeping*.] Is he, also, to take me walking on the boulevard? Is he to accompany me to the club and to the theatre?
[*Sobbing*].
SALOME. Be quiet! Enough! Give yourself no unnecessary heartache.

NATO [*jumps up and embraces Salome*]. Dear, dear mamma! dearest mamma, save me!

SALOME. Oh, rather would your mother be dead than to see this day!

NATO. Dear mamma, save me! save me, or I shall go into consumption! God is my witness!

SALOME [*weeping*]. The deuce take everything!
[*Wipes away her tears*].

NATO. Mamma, if you please, I would rather not marry at all. I will serve you here at home like a housemaid. Only make them stop this affair!

SALOME. That has already happened, my child.

NATO. Dear mamma, please do it.

SALOME. But I tell you, truly.

NATO. Is it really true?

SALOME. As true as the sun shines.

NATO [*kissing Salome*]. O my dear, dear mamma!

SALOME. At last I am rid of you. Your eyes are real tear-fountains. It would not have taken much more to make me cry, too.

NATO [*laughing*]. Ha! ha! ha!

SALOME. You can laugh now.

NATO. Ha! ha! ha! you gave me such a fright!

SALOME. You are terribly flighty. [*Presses the money into her hand.*] Here, take it; and do not be too long. [*Smoothes Nato's hair*].

NATO [*pulling herself away from her mother*]. Very well, mamma.
[*Taking her parasol and mantle*].

SALOME. Wipe your eyes, I pray, or they will laugh at you!

NATO. They are quite dry; and what does anybody care about my eyes?
[*Going*].

SALOME. Come back soon; don't allow yourself to be delayed.

NATO. I will come back right away, dear mamma.
[*Goes toward the right into the ante-room*].

Scene IV

SALOME [*alone*]. No, there is no other way out. Cost what it will, I shall accomplish what I want. Yes, I must, if I am ruined by it. Mother of God, plead for my Nato!

OSSEP [*enters, right*]. Where has Nato gone?

SALOME. Just across the way, to the store. She needed some music.

OSSEP. These are fine times for me! And a girl like this is to become a good citizen's wife!
[*Sits down on the sofa*].

SALOME [*coming near*]. That is what I say, too, dear Ossep. [*Lays hand on his shoulder.*] Are you not sorry? Is it not too bad about her?

OSSEP. I am still more to be pitied; but who pities me?
SALOME. Shall we really give her to a business man for a wife?

OSSEP. And what else? Is a merchant such a bad fellow? To judge by your words, I also am good for nothing; I who, day and night, worry myself to get you bread.

SALOME [*embracing him*]. How can you say such a thing, dear Ossep? Listen to me; are you not sorry for Nato? It would be quite different if she had been educated as I was.

OSSEP [*smiling*]. Hm! Then she would be the right sort.

SALOME [*draws back her hand*]. You are very polite, really! You laugh at poor me! Well, talk as you like, but finish this affair with Nato.

OSSEP. I have already finished it. What will you have of me?

SALOME. How, then? You will not give as much as they demand.

OSSEP. How can I give it when I have not so much?

SALOME [*embracing him*]. Dear Ossep, please do it.

OSSEP. But I cannot do it.

93

SALOME [*still pleading*]. If you love me only a little bit, you will do me this favor.

OSSEP. O woman! Can you not understand at all what yes and no mean? I tell you short and plain that I cannot afford to do it. My back is too weak to lift such a burden. A man can stretch out his feet in bed only as far as the covers reach. Isn't that true? Am I stingy? And would I be stingy toward my own child?

SALOME. But in this case no one asks whether we have it or not. Would it not be stupid to have such a lover for your daughter and not sacrifice everything for him? Others, indeed, have no great wealth, and yet give and are not called crazy.

OSSEP. Perhaps they have stolen money, since it is so easy for them to give it up. However, what is the use of so much talk? Take the cotton out of your ears and listen, for, I tell you, I have no money; and I repeat, I have no money. To-day or to-morrow I expect the conclusion of important business. If it is not completed, I am lost, body and soul. And you stand before me and torture me by asking me to do what is impossible!

SALOME. But why do you seem so angry? One cannot even open one's mouth before you.
[*Seats herself sulking on the tachta*].

OSSEP. Yes, I am angry. You women would exasperate an angel, let alone a man!

SALOME [*reproachfully*]. Just heaven! with my heart bleeding, I speak to you of our daughter and you are angry! You, then, are her father? Let us suppose I was dead: would it not be your sacred duty to provide for her future?

OSSEP. Am I not providing for her, you wicked woman? Have I not presented three or four young persons to you as sons-in-law? For that matter, they would still be very glad to

94

take her. They are young, clever, and industrious, and, moreover, persons of our condition in life. But who can be reasonable and speak to you? You have got it into your head that Nato's husband shall be an official, and there you stick. It is not your daughter's future that makes your heart bleed, but your own ambition.

SALOME. What more can I say to you? Are they, then, your equals? Who are they, properly speaking? Who are their parents?

OSSEP [*springing up*]. And who are you, then? Whose daughter, whose wife are you? Perhaps you are descended from King Heraclius; or perhaps you are the wife of a prince!

SALOME. How the man talks! Were your parents of better rank than mine? What? Say!

Scene V
Chacho

CHACHO [*enters, left*]. What's all this noise about?

OSSEP. O aunt, you are here?

CHACHO. Yes, it is I, as I love and live. How are you, my son?

OSSEP. Pretty well, thank God. And how are you, aunt?

CHACHO. My dear son, I am very feeble. But what is going on here? They must have heard your voices in the street.

SALOME. Do you not know that married people often have little quarrels?

CHACHO. That I know a hundred times better than you. And only a blockhead takes a dispute between man and wife

95

seriously. That is true; but that you two have already had time to get used to each other is also true.

OSSEP. Sit down, dear aunt. Tell me, rather, whether a wagon can be moved when one ox pulls to the right and the other to the left.

CHACHO. It will not stir from its place any more than I will now. [*Sits down with legs planted firmly.*] What can move me away from here?

OSSEP. Now, is it not true? One must help the other, for one alone cannot accomplish much, be he ever so strong and ready to work.

SALOME. Oh, yes! and you are the one ready to work and I am the lazy one, I suppose.

OSSEP. For heaven's sake, do not fly into a passion like that!

CHACHO [*to Salome*]. That was nothing more than a figure of speech. Who is accusing you of laziness?

OSSEP [*sitting down*]. Tell me, can we count ourselves among those persons who can give their daughter 10,000 rubles for a dowry? Are we able to do that?

SALOME. Eight thousand is surely not 10,000.

OSSEP. Both are too much for me.

SALOME. Oh, it is all the same to me; it is not for myself; it is for your daughter.
[*Sits down, ready to cry, upon the sofa*].
OSSEP. It is a beautiful thing, the way you look out for your daughter; but everything has its time and place. We have, remember, two other daughters to provide for.

CHACHO. Dear Ossep, why are you so obstinate?

OSSEP. I am not obstinate; but you two are. Yes, you are obstinate, and will pay no attention at all to what I say.

CHACHO. Since when have you become such a niggard? You should have economized when you gave the sasandars [41] something like ten rubles for a fee.

OSSEP. Those times have passed and won't come back again, dear aunt. At that time I was able to do it; but not now. Trade is dull and my business is going badly.

CHACHO. Possibly with your enemies, dear son; but there is nothing the matter with your business.

OSSEP [*aside*]. There you have it! They insist that I let them inspect my books. [*Aloud.*] Do you know, what, aunt? What I say I first consider, for I do not like to speak to no purpose. If that young man pleases you and my daughter, and you will have him at all hazards, I have nothing against it. So therefore go to him; and if you can settle the affair with 6,000 rubles, do it. I will gladly make the best of it; but mind, this is my last word, and if you hang me up by the feet, I will not add a single shilling.

CHACHO. What has come over you, Ossep? If you are willing to give 6,000 rubles, you will surely not let the whole thing go to pieces for the sake of 500 or 1,000 more?

OSSEP. Do you know what, aunt? Even if a voice from heaven were to demand it of me, that is my last word. Even if you flayed me alive, I would not give another shilling.

CHACHO. Do not excite yourself, dear son. Let us first see. Perhaps it can be settled with 6,000 rubles.

OSSEP. Yes, to that even I say yes.

SALOME. If a man can give 6,000, he can surely give 1,000 or 2,000 more. Why do you fret yourself unnecessarily?

---

[41] Musicians.

OSSEP [*aroused*]. God deliver me from the hands of these women! They say that one woman can get the best of two men; and here I am alone and fallen into the hands of two of you. Where, then, have you discovered this confounded fellow of a son-in-law? That comes of his visits. What has he to do with us? We are entirely different kind of people. [*To Salome:*] He is neither your brother nor your cousin; why, then, does he come running into our house? I believe he has been here as many as three times. I decline once and for all his visits. May his foot never cross my threshold!

CHACHO. Do not get excited, my son. Do not be vexed.

OSSEP. Now, aunt, you come so seldom to our house, and just to-day you happen in: how does that come?

CHACHO. If you are so vexed about my visit, go down in the cellar and cool yourself off a little.

OSSEP. I am a man; do you understand me? If I tell you that I can give no more, you should believe me.

CHACHO. We believe it, truly; we believe it, but we must say to you, nevertheless, that the dowry that a man gives his daughter means a great deal. It does not mean buying a house, when it is laudable to be economical. No; where the dowry is concerned, a man must think neither of his pocket nor of his money-box. You were acquainted with Jegor? Did he not sell his last house and afterward lived like a beggar to give his daughter a proper dowry? When he died, was there not money for his burial? That you know yourself very well. Are you any poorer than he, that you grumble like a bear about 2,000 rubles?

OSSEP. O great Heavens! they will bring me to despair yet. Isn't this a punishment of Providence, to bring up a daughter, spend a lot of money on her education, and when you have done everything, then hang a bag of gold around her neck, so that she may find someone who is kind enough to take her home with him? A pretty custom!

SALOME. Against the manners and customs of the world you can do nothing, however.

OSSEP. The devil take your manners and customs! If you hold so fast to old ways, then stick to all of them. Is it an old custom to wear, instead of Georgian shoes, little boots—and with men's heels, too? And that a girl should be ashamed to go with her own people and should walk around on the arm of a strange young man: is that also one of the good old customs? Where can we find anything of the good old manners and customs of our fathers, in the living or eating or housekeeping, or in the clothing, or in balls and society? What! was it so in old times? Do you still talk about old manners and customs? If once we begin to live after the new fashion, let us follow it in all things. Why do we still need to have bedclothes for twenty-four beds for guests? Why do we use the old cupboard and cake-oven and sofa-cover? Why does one not visit a mother with a young baby and stay whole months with them? Why does one invite 100 persons to a wedding and give funeral feasts and let eighty women mourners come and howl like so many dervishes? And what is that yonder [*points to the furniture*]? That one is old-fashioned and the others new-fashioned. If we can have one kind, why do we use the other?
[*Silent awhile*].

SALOME. Well, well! don't be angry! So you will give 6,000 rubles—you have promised it. What is lacking I will procure.

OSSEP. You will procure it? Where, then, will you get it? Not some of your own dowry, I hope.

SALOME. I had no dowry. Why do you tease me with that? No, everything I have I will sell or pawn. The pearls, my gold ornaments, I will take off of my *katiba*. The gold buttons can be melted. My brooch and my necklace, with twelve strings of pearls, I will also sell; and, if it is necessary, even the gold pins from my velvet cap must go. Let it all go! I will sacrifice everything for my Nato. I would give my head to keep the young man from slipping through my hands.
[Exit hastily at left].

Scene VI
Ossep. Chacho.

OSSEP. Have you ever seen anything like it, aunt? I ask you, aunt, does that seem right?

CHACHO. My son, who takes a thing like that to heart?

OSSEP. She is obstinate as a mule. Say, does she not deserve to be soundly beaten, now?

CHACHO. It only needed this—that you should say such a thing! As many years as you have lived together you have never harmed a hair of her head; then all of a sudden you begin to talk like this. Is that generous?

OSSEP. O aunt! I have had enough of it all. Were another man in my place, he would have had a separation long ago. [*Sits down.*] If she sees on anyone a new dress that pleases her, I must buy one like it for her; if a thing pleases her anywhere in a house, she wants one in her house; and if I don't get it for her she loses her senses. It is, for all the world, as though she belonged to the monkey tribe. Can a man endure it any longer?

CHACHO. The women are all so, my son. Why do you fret yourself so much on that account?

OSSEP. Yes, yes; you have the habit of making out that all women are alike—all! all! If other people break their heads against a stone, shall I do the same? No; I do what pleases myself, and not what pleases others.
CHACHO. Ossep, what nonsense are you talking? As I was coming here, even, I saw a laborer's wife so dressed up that a princess could hardly be compared with her. She had on a lilac silk dress and a splendid shawl on her head, fine, well-fitting gloves, and in her hand she held a satin parasol. I stood staring, open-mouthed, as she passed. Moreover, she trailed behind her a train three yards long. I tell you my heart was sad when I saw how she swept the street with that beautiful dress and dragged along all sorts of rubbish with it.

100

I really do not see why they still have street-sweepers. It was a long time before I could turn my eyes from her, and thought to myself, Lord, one can't tell the high from the low nowadays! And what can one say to the others if a laborer's wife puts on so much style?

OSSEP. I said that very thing. I have just spoken of it. A new public official has just arrived. She sees that others want to marry their daughters to him, and she runs, head first, against the wall to get ahead of them.

CHACHO. You are really peculiar. You have, you say, not enough money to provide a dowry for your daughter, and yet you brought her up and educated her in the fashion. For what has she learned to play the piano, then? Consider everything carefully.

OSSEP. Devil take this education! Of what good is this education if it ruins me? Is that sort of an education for the like of us? Ought we not to live as our fathers lived and stay in our own sphere, so that we could eat our bread with a good appetite? What kind of a life is that of the present day? Where is the appetizing bread of earlier times? Everything that one eats is smeared with gall! For what do I need a *salon* and a parlor, a cook and a footman? If a man stretches himself too much in his coat the seams must burst!

CHACHO. If you don't want to have all those things can't you manage the house another way? Who is to blame for it?

OSSEPO Have I managed it so? I wish he may break his neck who brought it all to pass! I haven't done it; it came of itself, and how it happened I don't know Oftentimes when I look back over my early days I see that things were very different twenty years ago. It seems to me I have to live like an ambassador! [*Stands up.*] We are all the same, yes, we all go the same pace. Wherever you go you find the same conditions, and no one questions whether his means permit it. If a man who has 10,000 rubles lives so, I say nothing; but if one with an income of 1,000 rubles imitates him, then my good-nature stops. What are the poorer people to learn from us if we give them such an example? Weren't the old times much better? In a single *darbas* [42] we all lived together; three or four brothers and their families. We saved in light and heat, and the blessing of God was with us. Now in that respect it is wholly different. If one brother spends fifty rubles, the other spends double the sum, so as not to be behind him. And what kind of brothers are there now, as a rule? And what kind of sisters and fathers and mothers? If you were to chain them together you could not hold them together a week at a time. If it is not a punishment from God, I don't know what is.

CHACHO. My dear Ossep, why do you revive those old memories? It gives me the heartache to recall those old times. I remember very well how it was. In the room stood a long broad sofa that was covered with a carpet. When evening came there would be a fire-pan lighted in the middle of the room and we children would sit around it That was our chandelier. Then a blue table-cloth was spread on the sofa and something to eat, and everything that tasted good in those days was placed on it. Then we sat around it, happy as could be: grandfather, father, uncle, aunt, brothers, and sisters. The wine pitcher poured out sparkling wine into the glasses, and it wandered from one end of the table to the other. Many times there were twenty of us. Now if for any reason five persons come together in a room one is likely to be suffocated. [*Points to the ceiling.*] With us there was an opening for smoke in the ceiling that was worth twenty windows. When it became bright in the morning the daylight pressed in on us, and when it grew dark the twilight came in there, and the stars glimmered through. Then we spread our bed-things out, and we went to sleep together with play and frolic. We had a kettle and a roasting-spit in the house, and also a pot-ladle and strainer, and the men brought in the stock of provisions in bags. Of the things they brought, one thing was as appetizing as the other. Now, it seems the cooks and servants eat all the best bits. God preserve me from them! Our homes are ruined by the new ways!

---

[42] Hall.

OSSEP. Do you know what, aunt? I wager it will not be long before the whole city is bankrupt. On one side extravagance and the new mode of life will be to blame, and on the other our stupidity. Can we go on living so? It is God's punishment, and nothing more. You will scarcely believe it when I tell you that I pay out ten rubles every month for pastry for the children alone.

CHACHO. No! Reduce your expenses a little, my son. Retrench!

OSSEP. That is easily said. Retrench, is it? Well, come over here and do it. I would like to see once how you would begin. Listen, now! Lately I bought a pair of children's shoes at the bazaar for three abaces. [43] The lad threw them to the ceiling. "I want boots at two and a half rubles," said the six-year-old rascal. He was ready to burst out crying. What could I do but buy new ones? If others would do the same I could let the youngster run in cheap boots. How can one retrench here? Twenty years, already, I have struggled and see no way out. To-day or to-morrow my head will burst, or I may beat it to pieces against a stone wall. Isn't it an effort at retrenchment when I say that I cannot afford it? but with whom am I to speak here? Does anyone understand me? Yes, reduce your expenses!
[*Goes toward the ante-room to the right and meets Nato with four sheets of music in her hand*].

Scene VII
Nato, Ossep, Chacho.

OSSEP. Yes, yes, reduce your expenses!

CHACHO. Little girl, how quickly you have come back!

NATO. I did not go far, aunt.

CHACHO. What have you in your hand, sweetheart?

---

[43] Abace—20 kopecks.

103

NATO. I have bought some new music.

OSSEP [*stepping up to them*]. Yes, yes, retrench! [*Taking a sheet of music out of her hand.*] What did you pay for this?

NATO. Four abaces.

OSSEP. And for this [*taking another*]?

NATO [*looking at it*]. Six abaces.

OSSEP [*taking a third*]. And for this?

NATO [*fretfully*]. One ruble and a half.

OSSEP [*taking the last*]. And certainly as much for this?

NATO. No, papa; I paid two rubles and a half for that.

OSSEP [*angrily*]. And one is to economize! Am I to blame for this? What have you bought four pieces for? Was not one or two enough?

NATO [*frightened*]. I need them.

OSSEP [*still more angrily*]. Tell me one thing—is this to be endured? If she could play properly at least, but she only drums two or three pieces and says she can play. I cannot play myself, but I have heard persons who played well. They could use these things, but not we. I wish the devil had the man who introduced this! [*Throws the music on the floor.*] I'll cut off my hand if she can play properly.

CHACHO. There, there, stop, now!

OSSEP. Whatever she tries to do is only half done: music, languages—she has only half learned. Tell me, what can she do? Is she able to sew anything? or to cut out a dress for herself? Yes, that one seems like a European girl! Ha! ha! Five times I have been in Leipsic, and the daughter of the merest pauper there can do more than she can. What have I

104

not seen in the way of needlework! I gaped with admiration. And she cannot even speak Armenian properly, and that is her mother tongue! Can she write a page without mistakes? Can she pronounce ten French words fluently? Yes, tell me, what can she do? What does she understand? She will make a fine housekeeper for you! The man who takes her for his wife is to be pitied. She be able to share with him the troubles of life! Some day or other she will be a mother and must bring up children. Ha, ha! they will have a fine bringing-up! She is here to make a show; but for nothing beside! She is an adept at spending money. Yes, give her money, money, so that she can rig herself out and go to balls and parties! [*Nato cries.*] Can I stand this any longer? Can I go on with these doings? Retrench, you say. What is this [*taking a corner of Nato's tunic in his hand*]? How is this for a twelve-story building? Does it warm the back? How am I to reduce expenses here? And if I do it, will others do it also? I'd like to see the man who could do it!
[*Nato still crying*].

CHACHO. Do all these things you have said in my presence amount to anything? You yourself said that you troubled yourself little about what others did. What do you want, then? Why should you poison the heart of this innocent girl? [*All are silent awhile*].

OSSEP [*lays his hand on his forehead and recovers himself.*] O just heaven, what am I doing? I am beside myself. [*Goes up to Nato.*] Not to you, not to you, my Nato, should I say all this! [*Embraces her.*] No, you do not deserve it; you are innocent. We are to blame for all. I am to blame, I! because I imitated the others and brought you up as others brought up their daughters. Don't cry! I did not wish to hurt you. I was in bad humor, for everything has vexed me to-day, and unfortunately you came in at the wrong moment. [*Picks up the music and gives it to her.*] Here, take the music, my child. [*Embraces her again.*] Go and buy some more. Do what you wish everywhere, and be behind no one. Until to-day you have wanted nothing, and, with God's help, you shall want nothing in the future.
[*Kisses her and turns to go*].

CHACHO. Now, Ossep, think it over; come to some decision in the matter.

OSSEP. I should like to, indeed; but what I cannot do I cannot do.
[*Goes off at the right*].

Scene VIII
Nato, Chacho, then Salome.

NATO [*falling sobbing in Chacho's arms*]. O dear, dear aunt.

CHACHO. Stop; don't cry, my dear, my precious child. It is indeed your father. Stop; stop, Salome.

SALOME [*coming in smiling*]. Dear aunt, I have arranged everything. [*Stops.*] What is this now? Why are you crying? [*Nato wipes away her tears and goes toward the divan*].

CHACHO. You know her father, don't you? He has been scolding her, and has made her cry.

SALOME. If her father has been troubling her, then I will make her happy again. Nato, dear, I have betrothed you. [*Nato looks at her in wonderment.*] Yes, my love, be happy—what have you to say about it? Mr. Alexander Marmarow is now your betrothed.

NATO. Is it really true, mamma dear?

CHACHO [*at the same time*]. Is it true?

SALOME. It is true, be assured.

NATO [*embracing Salome*]. O my dear, dear mother.

SALOME [*seizing her daughter and kissing her*]. Now I am
106

rid of my worries about you. I hope it will bring you joy. Go and put on another dress, for your betrothed is coming.

NATO. Now?

SALOME. Certainly, at once. You know, I presume, that you must make yourself pretty.

NATO [*happy and speaking quickly*]. Certainly. I will wear the white barège with blue ribbons, the little cross on black velvet ribbon, and a blue ribbon in my hair. [*Hugs Chacho.*] O my precious auntie!

CHACHO [*embracing and kissing her*]. May this hour bring you good-fortune! I wish it for you with all my heart.

NATO [*hugging and kissing Salome again*]. O you dear, you dearest mamma.
[*Runs out of the room*].

Scene IX
Salome. Chacho.

CHACHO. What does all this mean? Am I dreaming or am I still awake?

SALOME. What are you saying about dreams? His sister Champera was here, and about five minutes later he himself came. They live very near here.

CHACHO. If it was arranged so easily, why have you wrangled and quarrelled so much?

SALOME [*in a whisper*]. But what do you think, aunt? I have arranged the affair for 7,000 rubles, and I have had to promise his sister 200 rubles beside.

CHACHO. May I be struck blind! And you have done this without Ossep's knowing it?

107

SALOME [*whispering*]. He will not kill me for it, and let him talk as much as he will. It could not go through otherwise. Get up and let us go into that room where Ossep will not hear us.
[*Helps her to rise*].

CHACHO. O just heaven! What women we have in these days!

Scene X

OSSEP [*alone, buckling his belt and holding his cap in his hand, comes in through the right-hand door, stands awhile in deep thought while he wrings his hands several times*]. Give me money! Give me money! I would like to know where I am to get it. It is hard for me to give what I have promised. And what if it cannot be arranged for that sum? Am I, then, to make a mess of this!—I who have always been willing to make any sacrifice for my children? It must, indeed, lie in this—that the suitor does not please; for I could not find 2,000 to add to the 6,000 that I have promised. Yes, that's it! The man is not the one I want for her. If he were an ordinary fellow, he would not treat with me. At any rate, what he is after will show itself now; yes, we shall soon see what kind of man he is! Up to this day I have always kept my word, and the best thing I can do is to keep it now.

Enter Gewo.

OSSEP [*meeting him as he enters from the right*]. Oh, it is you, dear Gewo! What brings you to our house? [*Offering him his hand.*] I love you; come again, and often!

GEWO. You know well that if I had not need of you, I would not come.

OSSEP. How can I serve you? Pray, sit down.

GEWO [*seating himself*]. What are you saying about serving? Do you think that this confounded Santurian has—

108

OSSEP [*interrupting him anxiously*]. What has happened?

GEWO. The dear God knows what has happened to the fellow!

OSSEP. But go on, what has happened?

GEWO. What could happen? The fellow has cleared out everything.

OSSEP [*disturbed and speaking softly*]. What did you say, Gewo? Then I am lost, body and soul; then I am ruined!

GEWO. I hope he will go to the bottom. How is one to trust any human being nowadays? Everyone who saw his way of living must have taken him for an honest man.

OSSEP [*softly*]. You kill me, man!

GEWO. God in heaven should have destroyed him long ago, so that this could not have happened. But who could have foreseen it? When one went into his store everything was always in the best order. He kept his word, paid promptly when the money was due; but what lay behind that, no one knew.

OSSEP. I have depended on him so much. What do you say, Gewo? He owes me 10,000 rubles! I was going to satisfy my creditors with this sum. To-morrow his payment was due, and the next day mine. How can I satisfy them now? Can I say that I cannot pay them because Santurian has given me nothing? Am I to be a bankrupt as well as he? May the earth swallow me rather!

GEWO. I wish the earth would swallow him, or rather that he had never come into the world! I have just 2,000 rubles on hand; if you wish I will give them to you to-morrow.

OSSEP. Good; I will be very thankful for them. But what do you say to that shameless fellow? Have you seen him? Have you spoken with him?

GEWO. Of course. I have just come from him.

OSSEP. What did he say? Will he really give nothing?

GEWO. If he does not lie, he will settle with you alone. Let the others kick, he said. Go to him right off, dear Ossep. Before the thing becomes known perhaps you can still get something out of him.

OSSEP. Come with me, Gewo. Yes, we must do something, or else I am lost.

GEWO. The devil take the scoundrel!

Scene XI

SALOME [*coming in from the left*]. May I lose my sight if he is not coming already. He is already on the walk. [*Looking out of the window and then walking toward the entry.*] How my heart beats!
[*Goes into the ante-room. Alexander appears at the window and then at the door of the ante-room.*]

Alexander enters.

SALOME [*at the door*]. Come; pray come in. [*Offers her hand.*] May your coming into our house bring blessings!

ALEXANDER [*making a bow*]. Madame Salome [*kisses her hand*], I am happy that from now on I dare call myself your son.

SALOME [*kissing him on the brow*]. May God make you as happy as your mother wishes. Please, please sit down! Nato will be here immediately.
[*They sit down*].

ALEXANDER. How are you, Madame Salome? What is Miss Natalie doing? Since that evening I have not had the pleasure of seeing her.

110

SALOME. Thank you, she is very well. The concert that evening pleased me exceedingly. Thank heaven that so good a fashion has found entrance among us. In this way we have a perfect bazaar for the marriageable girls, for had not this concert taken place where would you two have found an opportunity to make each other's acquaintance? Where else could you have caught sight of each other?

ALEXANDER. Dear lady, Miss Natalie must please everybody without concerts, and awaken love in them. Oh, how I bless my fate that it is my happy lot to win her love!

SALOME. And my Nato pleases you, dear son-in-law?

ALEXANDER. Oh, I love her with all my heart, dear madame!

SALOME. If you love her so much, dear son, why did you exact so much money? For the sake of 1,000 rubles this affair almost went to pieces. Your sister Champera swore to me that if we did not give 1,000 rubles more you would this very day betroth yourself to the daughter of Barssegh Leproink.

ALEXANDER. I wonder, Madame Salome, that you should credit such things. I marry Leproink's daughter! I refuse Miss Natalie on her account! forget her beautiful black eyes and her good heart, and run after money! Would not that be shameful in me! I must confess to you freely, dear madame, that my sister's way of doing things is hateful to me. *Fi mauvais genre!* But let us say no more about it. If only God will help us to a good ending!

SALOME. God grant that neither of you may have anything to regret!—[*rising*] I will come back immediately, dear son-in-law; I am only going to see what is keeping Nato. [*Alexander also rises.*] Keep your seat, I beg of you. How ceremonious you are! I will come right back. [*Exit right*].

111

Scene XII

ALEXANDER [*alone.*] At last my burning wish is fulfilled! Now I have both a pretty wife and money. Without money a man is not of the least importance. Let him give himself what trouble he may, if he has no money, no one will pay any attention to him. I have made only one mistake in the business. I have been in too much of a hurry. If I had held out a little longer they would have given me 8,000 rubles; now I must be satisfied with 7,000. Still, what was to be done? It would not have gone through otherwise; and for that matter, I may, perhaps, somehow make up for it in other ways. In any case, I stand here on a fat pasture-land where they seem to be pretty rich. The principal thing is that I should make myself popular among them, then I shall have succeeded in getting my fill out of them. Ha, ha, ha! How they worry themselves! Yes, the whole office will be in an uproar to-morrow. [*With affected voice:*] "Have you heard the news? Marmarow is engaged, and has received 7,000 rubles dowry. And such a beautiful girl! Such a lovely creature!" [*Clucking with his tongue and changing his voice:*] "Is it possible!" [*In his own voice:*] Charming, charming, Marmarow! [*Looking at his clothing:*] Chic! A true gentleman am I! Yes, I am getting on. I must now think only of to-morrow and the next day, and how to get on further. The principal thing is for a man to know the value of money, for without money nothing can be undertaken. First, I shall have the interest on my capital; then my salary, and last some hundred rubles beside. That makes 3,000 or 4,000 rubles a year. If I lay aside 1,000 rubles every year, I have in seven or eight years 10,000; in fifteen years double that, and so on. Yes, Monsieur Marmarow, you understand it! Be happy, therefore, and let the others burst with envy. *Salome and Nato enter at the right, Salome holding Nato's hand.*

ALEXANDER. Miss Natalie, the whole night long I thought only of you! [*Kisses her hand.*]

SALOME. Kiss her on the cheek and give her the engagement ring.

ALEXANDER. Oh, you are the sun of my existence! [*Draws a ring from his finger and gives it to Natalie.*] From now on you are mine. Please! [*Kisses her.*]

SALOME. Be happy and may you reach old age together. [*Kisses Alexander; then Nato.*] God bless you, my children. Sit down, I pray you, Alexander [*pointing to the sofa on which Alexander and Nato sit down*]. Your father will soon be here. [*Walks to and fro in joyful excitement.*]

ALEXANDER [*looking at Nato*]. Dear Natalie, why are you so silent? Let me hear your sweet voice, I beg of you.

NATO. I am speechless, Monsieur Marmarow.

ALEXANDER. Monsieur!

NATO. Dear Alexander.

ALEXANDER [*seizing her hand*]. So! That sounds much sweeter! [*Kisses her hand.*]

Enter Chacho.

SALOME. Come in, dear aunt.

CHACHO. Such a thing has never happened to me before! Could you not wait till the man of the house arrived?

SALOME. Oh, it is all the same; he will be here soon enough. Give them your blessing, I beg of you.

CHACHO. May God bestow all good things upon you. May heaven grant the prayer of me, a sinner. [*Alexander and Nato stand up.*] May you have nothing to regret. May you flourish and prosper and grow old together on the same pillow. [*Ossep comes to the door and stands astonished.*]

CHACHO [*continuing*]. God grant that your first may be a boy! Love and respect each other! May the eye of the

113

Czar look down on you with mercy! [*Sees Ossep.*]
Let the father now offer you his good wishes.

SALOME. Dear Ossep, congratulate your daughter.

NATO. Dear papa!
[*Goes up to Ossep and kisses his hand. Ossep stands motionless*].

ALEXANDER [*seizing Ossep's hand*]. From now on, dear father, count me among your children. [*Turning to Nato offended*:] What is this?

SALOME. Don't be impolite, Ossep.

CHACHO. What has happened to you, Ossep?

ALEXANDER [*to Salome*]. I understand nothing of this. [*To Ossep*:] My father, you seem dissatisfied.

OSSEP [*recovering himself*]. I dissatisfied! No—yes—I am dizzy.

ALEXANDER [*offering him a chair*]. Sit down, I pray, my father.

OSSEP [*to Alexander*]. Do not trouble yourself. It is already passed.

SALOME. Can one meet his son-in-law like that? And such a son-in-law, beside! Say something, do.

OSSEP. What shall I say, then? You have consummated the betrothal. God grant that all will end well. [*To Alexander*:] Please be seated.

ALEXANDER. My father, when do you wish the betrothal to be celebrated?

OSSEP. That depends upon you. Do as you wish.

ALEXANDER. I will invite twenty persons and bring them with me. My superiors I must invite also; it would not do to omit them.

OSSEP. Do as you see fit.

ALEXANDER [*to Salome*]. Perhaps he is angry with me. If there is any reason for it, pray tell me now.

SALOME. What are you saying? That cannot be!
[*They move away a little and speak softly together.*]

OSSEP [*on the other side of the stage to Chacho*]. You Godforsaken! Could you not wait a moment?

CHACHO. What is the matter now?

OSSEP. Only God in heaven knows how I stand! Think of it! Santurian has failed.

CHACHO. Great heaven!

ALEXANDER [*offering Nato his arm*]. Something must have happened! [*They go off at the left, Salome following.*]

OSSEP. Righteous God, why dost thou punish me thus?

SALOME [*returning to Ossep*]. Do with me as you will, but it could not have been helped. I have promised him 7,000 rubles as dowry, [*Turning to Chacho as she leaves the room:*] Pray come with me, aunt. You come, too, Ossep. [*Exit Salome*].

Scene XIII

OSSEP [*much excited*]. What do I hear? Has she spoken the truth? Do you hear? Why do you not answer me? Why are you silent? [*Still more excited.*] It is true, then! Yes, yes, I see that it is true! O God, let lightning strike this unlucky house that we may all die together. I have just lost an important sum and come home to prevent further negotiations. And see there!

CHACHO. I am to blame for it. Do not get excited. I will add 1,000 rubles to it, if need be, from the money I have laid by for my burial.

OSSEP. From your burial money? Have I already fallen so low that I must ask alms? Keep your money for yourself! I do not want it. Drop that complaint also, for I am still rich, very rich. How can it injure me that Santurian has failed? I stand here firm and unshakable, and have inexhaustible money resources. [*Tearing his hair.*] O God! O God! [*Walks to and fro excitedly.*] Now I will go and wish my son-in-law joy. Yes, I must go so that I shall not make myself ridiculous to him. The man is a government official!
[*Exit right, laughing bitterly.*]

CHACHO. Gracious heaven, be thou our saviour and deliverer.

CURTAIN.

ACT SECOND

Scene I

A richly furnished sales-room in Barssegh's house.

MICHO. Two, three, four, five, six and this little piece. It does not measure so much!

BARSSEGH [*standing up and giving Micho a rap on the nose*]. You have what is lacking there. Measure again. Now you've got what is lacking. I will tear your soul out of your body if you measure so that in seven arschin 44 it comes out one werschok short.

MICHO [*measuring again*]. O dear, O dear!

BARSSEGH. Look out, or I will take that "O dear" out of your ear. Be up and at it now!

MICHO. Oh, Mr. Barssegh! [*Measuring.*] One, two, three—

BARSSEGH. Stretch it, you blockhead.

MICHO [*stretching the cotton*]. Three, four. [*Wipes the perspiration from his brow.*]

BARSSEGH. What is the matter with you? You sweat as though you had a mule-pack on your back.

MICHO. Five.

BARSSEGH. Pull it out more.

MICHO. Six and this little piece. It lacks three werschok again.

BARSSEGH [*pulling his ears*]. It lacks three werschok? There they are!

MICHO. Oh my, oh my!

BARSSEGH. You calf; will you ever develop into a man?

MICHO. O dear mother!

BARSSEGH [*pulling him again by the ear*]. Doesn't it grow longer?

MICHO [*crying*]. Dear Mr. Barssegh, dear sir, let me go.

---

44 Russian measure of length.

117

BARSSEGH. I want to teach you how to measure.

MICHO. It reaches, I say; it reaches, indeed; it reaches. Let me measure again.

BARSSEGH. Now take care that you make it seven arschin.

MICHO [*aside*]. Holy Karapet, help me. [*Measuring.*] One, two—

BARSSEGH. O you blockhead!

MICHO. Three.

BARSSEGH Wake up!

MICHO. Four.

BARSSEGH. Haven't you seen how Dartscho measures?

MICHO. Five.

BARSSEGH. Will you ever learn how to do it?

MICHO. Five.

BARSSEGH. If you keep on being so stupid my business will be ruined.

MICHO. Five—five.

BARSSEGH. I give you my word that I will give you the sack.

MICHO. Five—five.

BARSSEGH. Measure further.

MICHO. Five—[*aside*:]; Holy George, help me! [*Aloud*:] Six. I cannot stretch it any more or I shall tear it.

BARSSEGH. Measure, now.

MICHO. O dear; I believe it is already torn.

BARSSEGH [*looking at the cloth*]. I see nothing. God forbid!

MICHO [*looking at the measure*]. It is short a half werschok of seven arschin every time.
The madman, Mosi, comes in at the middle door and stands in the background

Scene II
Mosi.

BARSSEGH [*hitting Micho on the head*]. What are you good for? Can't you get that half werschok out of it?

MICHO [*howling.*] What am I to do when the cloth is too short?

BARSSEGH [*pulling his hair*]. Are you sure you're not lying?

MICHO [*yelling.*] How can you say that? Measure it yourself and we shall see whether there are seven arschin here.

BARSSEGH [*angry; taking measure and calico*]. You say there are not seven here? Wait, I will show you [*measuring.*] One, two, three, four, five, six, seven, and a quarter left over for a present to you. What do you say about it now? You must learn to measure if you burst doing it. But you think only of your week's pay. Now, hurry up; be lively there!

MICHO. O heaven! How shall I begin? One, two—

BARSSEGH. Be careful and don't tear it.

MICHO [*crying.*] What do you want of me? If I pull on the stuff I tear it; and if I don't stretch it, no seven arschin will come out of it.

MOSI [*coming near*]. Ha! ha! ha! Who is the toper? Who?

119

'Tis I; the mad Mosi. Ha! ha! ha!

BARSSEGH [*aside.*] How comes this crazy fellow here?

MOSI [*seizing the measure and calico*]. Give it to me, you booby! There are not only seven arschin here, but twenty-seven [*measuring quickly*]. One, two, four, six, eight, ten, twelve, and here are thirteen and fourteen. Do you want me to make still more out of it? You must shove the stick back in measuring. Can't you understand that? [*Throws the stick and calico upon Micho.*] Here, take it and be a man at last. You the shop-boy of such a great merchant and not find out a little thing like that. Haven't you learned yet how to steal half a werschok? Ha, ha, ha!
[*Micho tries to free himself but becomes more entangled in the cloth*].

BARSSEGH [*to Mosi*], I forbid such impudent talk in my presence! Be silent, or I'll show you.

MOSI. That's the way with all mankind. They never appreciate good intentions. [*Pointing to Micho.*] I only wanted to make something of him. Go, go, my son, be a man! Learn from your master! You surely see how much money he has scraped together! [*To Barssegh:*] How is it about eating? It's time for dinner! Have the table set; I have come as a guest. What have you to-day? Coal-soup, perhaps, or water-soup? Yes, yes; you will entertain me finely! Ha, ha!

BARSSEGH [*aside*]. This confounded fellow is drunk again! [*To Micho:*] Get out of the room!
[*Exit Micho middle door*].

Scene III

MOSI. From this stuff you can make a shroud for yourself. To-day or to-morrow you must die, that's sure.

BARSSEGH. You'd better be still!
[*Enter Khali at left*].

120

KHALI. Do you know the latest?

BARSSEGH. What has happened?

KHALI. What has happened? Marmarow was betrothed yesterday.

BARSSEGH. No!

KHALI. By heaven!

BARSSEGH. To whom?

KHALI. To the daughter of Ossep Gulabianz.

BARSSEGH. Is that really true?

KHALI. Do you think I am lying? They promised him 10,000 rubles dowry. I always said you should have saved something. Now you have it! They have snatched him away from you. And such a man, too! They puff themselves up entirely too much. Where did they get the money, I would like to know?
[*Micho appears at the middle door*].

BARSSEGH. Run right off down to the Tapitach. [45] You know where Ossep Gulabianz's store is?

MICHO. Gulabianz? The one who brought money to-day?

BARSSEGH. Yes, that one. Go and look for him wherever he is likely to be. Tell him he must bring the rest of the money at once. Now, run quickly. What else do I want to say? Oh, yes [*pointing to the calico*]; take that winding-sheet with you.

MOSI. Ha, ha, ha! Listen to him!

BARSSEGH. By heaven! What am I chattering about? I am

---

[45] A district of Tiflis.

crazed! [*Angrily, to Micho:*] What are you gaping at? Do you hear? Take this calico. Go to the store and tell Dartscho to come here. Lively, now!
[*Exit Micho with goods*].

BARSSEGH [*going on*]. I would like to see how he is going to give 10,000 rubles dowry. I would like to know whose money it is?

KHALI. That stuck-up Salome has gotten my son-in-law away from me.

BARSSEGH. Never mind. I will soon put them into a hole.

MOSI. Oh, don't brag about things you can't perform. What has Ossep done to you that you want revenge? How can Ossep help it if your daughter is as dumb as straw and has a mouth three ells long? And what have Micho's ears to do with it? You should simply have given what the man asked.

BARSSEGH [*rising*]. O you wretch, you!

MOSI. Yes, you should certainly have paid it. Why didn't you? For whom are you saving? To-morrow or the day after you will have to die and leave it here.

BARSSEGH. Stop, or—

KHALI [*to Mosi*]. Why do you anger him? Haven't we trouble and anxiety enough?

MOSI. Well, I will be still. But I swear that this young man may call himself lucky that he has freed himself from you and closed with Ossep. Both of you together are not worth Ossep's finger-tips.

BARSSEGH. Leave me in peace or I will shake off all my anger on to you.

MOSI. What can you do to me? You cannot put my store under the hammer. What a man you are, indeed!

122

BARSSEGH. A better man than you any day.

MOSI. In what are you better?

BARSSEGH. In the first place, I am master of my five senses, and you are cracked.

MOSI [*laughs*]. Ha, ha, ha! If you were rational you would not have said that. Am I crazy because I show up your villanies? You are wise, you say? Perhaps you are as wise as Solomon!

BARSSEGH. I am wealthy.

MOSI. Take your money and—[*Whispers something in his ear.*] You have stolen it here and there. You have swindled me out of something, too. Me and this one and that one, and so you became rich! You have provided yourself with a carriage, and go riding in it and make yourself important. Yes, that is the way with your money. Did your father Matus come riding to his store in a carriage, eh? You say you are rich? True, there is scarcely anyone richer than you; but if we reckon together all the money you have gained honorably, we shall see which of us two has most. [*Drawing his purse from his pocket and slapping it.*] See! I have earned all this by the sweat of my brow. Oh, no, like you I collected it for the church and put it in my own pocket. Are you going to fail again soon?

BARSSEGH. Heaven preserve me from it!

MOSI. It would not be the first time. When you are dead they will shake whole sacks full of money in your grave for you.

BARSSEGH. Will you never stop?

KHALI. Are you not ashamed to make such speeches?

MOSI. Till you die I will not let you rest. As long as you live I will gnaw at you like a worm, for you deserve it for your

123

villany. What! Haven't you committed every crime? You robbed your brother of his inheritance; you cheated your partner; you have repudiated debts, and held others to false debts. Haven't you set your neighbors' stores on fire? If people knew everything they would hang you. But the world is stone-blind, and so you walk God's earth in peace. Good-by! I would like to go to Ossep and warn him against you; for if he falls into your clutches he is lost.

Scene IV

BARSSEGH. Yes, yes; go and never come back.

KHALI. I wish water lay in front of him and a drawn sword behind.

BARSSEGH. This fellow is a veritable curse!

KHALI. Yes, he is, indeed.

BARSSEGH. The devil take him! If he is going to utter such slanders, I hope he will always do it here, and not do me harm with outsiders.

KHALI. You are to blame for it yourself. Why do you have anything to do with the good-for-nothing fellow?

BARSSEGH. There you go! Do I have anything to do with him? He is always at my heels, like my own shadow.

KHALI. Can't you forbid him to enter your doors?

BARSSEGH. So that he will not let me pass by in the streets? Do you want him to make me the talk of the town?

KHALI. Then don't speak to him any more.

BARSSEGH. As if I took pleasure in it! It is all the same to him whether one speaks to him or not.

KHALI. What are we to do with him, then?

BARSSEGH [*angrily*]. Why do you fasten yourself on to me like a gadfly? Have I not trouble enough already? [*Beating his hands together.*] How could you let him escape? You are good for nothing!

KHALI. What could I do, then, if you were stingy about the money? If you had promised the 10,000 rubles, you would have seen how easily and quickly everything would have been arranged.

BARSSEGH. If he insists upon so much he may go to the devil. For 10,000 rubles I will find a better man for my daughter.

KHALI. I know whom you mean. Give me the money and I will arrange the thing to-day.

BARSSEGH [*derisively*]. Give it! How easily you can say it! Is that a mulberry-tree, then, that one has only to shake and thousands will fall from it? Don't hold my rubles so cheaply; for every one of them I have sold my soul twenty times.

KHALI. If I can only get sight of that insolent Salome, I'll shake a cart-load of dirt over her head. Only let her meet me! [*Exit, left*].

Scene V

BARSSEGH [*alone*]. And you shall see what I will do! Only wait, my dear Ossep! I am getting a day of joy ready for you and you will shed tears as thick as my thumb. I have been looking for the chance a long time, and now fate has delivered you into my hands. You braggart, you shall see how you will lie at my feet. I am the son of the cobbler Matus. There are certain simpletons who shake their heads over those who had nothing and suddenly amount to something. But I tell you that this world is nothing more than a great honey-cask. He who carries away the best part for himself, without letting the others come near it, he is the man to whom praise and honor are due. But a man who stands aside, like Ossep, and waits till his turn comes is an ass.

Enter Dartscho.

BARSSEGH. Ah, Dartscho! How quickly you have come!

DARTSCHO. I met Micho just now, and he told me that you had sent for me.

BARSSEGH. I have something important to speak with you about. [*He sits down.*] Where were you just now?

DARTSCHO. At George's, the coal man. He owed us some money, and I have been to see him seven times this week on that account.

BARSSEGH. He is very unpunctual. But how does it stand? Has he paid?

DARTSCHO. Of course! What do you take me for? I stayed in the store as if nailed there, and when a new customer came in I repeated my demand. There was nothing left for him to do but to pay me, for shame's sake.

BARSSEGH. That pleases me in you, my son. Go on like that and you will get on in the world. Look at me! There was a time when they beat me over the head and called me by my given name. Then they called me Barssegh, and finally "Mr." Barssegh. When I was as old as you are I was nothing, and now I am a man who stands for something. If my father, Matus, were still alive he would be proud of me. I tell you all this so that you will spare no pains to make yourself a master and make people forget that you are the son of a driver. A son can raise up the name of his father; he can also drag it down into the dust.

DARTSCHO. You see best of all what trouble I take, Mr.

126

Barssegh. When I open the store in the morning, I never wait until Micho comes, but I take the broom in my hand and sweep out the store. And how I behave with the customers, you yourself see.

BARSSEGH. Yes, I see it; I see it, my son, and it is on that account I am so good to you. Only wait till next year and you shall be my partner. I will supply the money and you the labor.

DARTSCHO. May God give you a long life for that! I seem to myself like a tree which you have planted. I hope I will still bear fruit and you will have your joy in me. Do you know that I have gotten rid of those damaged goods?

BARSSEGH. Is it possible?

DARTSCHO. It's a fact.

BARSSEGH. To whom have you sold them?

DARTSCHO. To a man from Signach. I laid two good pieces on top so that he did not notice it. Let him groan now.

BARSSEGH. And how? On credit?

DARTSCHO. Am I then crazy? Have I ever sold damaged goods on credit, that you make such a supposition? Of course I took something off for it, but made believe I only did it to please him. He paid me the full sum at once; and if he is now boasting how cheap he bought the goods, I hope he will sing my praises also.

BARSSEGH. Do you know, dear Dartscho, you are a fine fellow? Yes, I have always said that you would amount to something.

DARTSCHO. God grant it! What commands have you, Mr. Barssegh? There is no one in the store.

BARSSEGH. Oh, right! I had almost forgotten. If Ossep

127

Gulabianz comes to borrow money, give him nothing.

DARTSCHO. What has happened?

BARSSEGH. I am terribly angry at him.

DARTSCHO. And I have even more reason to be angry at him; he is altogether too stuck-up. But what has occurred?

BARSSEGH. I will show him now who I am. His whole business is just like a hayrick; a match is enough to set the whole thing ablaze.

DARTSCHO. I would not be sorry for ten matches! Tell me what I can do about it? The rest I know already.

BARSSEGH. Think of it! The fellow has snatched away a fine fat morsel from my very mouth. I had found an excellent husband for my daughter. For a whole week we carried on negotiations with him and everything was near final settlement when this Ossep came in and bid over us. On the very same day he betrothed his daughter to the man.

DARTSCHO. The devil take him for it!

BARSSEGH. And do you know, also, whose money he is going to use? It is my money he is going to give him.

DARTSCHO. That is just it! That is it!

BARSSEGH. Things look bad for his pocket. Now he is going to marry off his daughter and put himself in a tight place. Go, therefore, and get out an execution against him; otherwise nothing can be squeezed out of him.

DARTSCHO. We shall see. I will go at once and demand our money.

BARSSEGH. I have already sent Micho, but I hardly believe he will give it up so easily. On that account I sent for you to find out someone who can help us.

DARTSCHO. I know a lawyer who can manage so that in three hours they will put an attachment on his store.

BARSSEGH. Go on so forever, dear Dartscho! Yes, I have long known that you were going to be the right sort of fellow!

DARTSCHO. The apprentice of a right good master always gets on in the world.

BARSSEGH. Go quickly then; lose no time.

DARTSCHO. I will not waste an hour.

BARSSEGH. Go! May you succeed!
[*Exit Dartscho, middle door*].

BARSSEGH [*alone*]. Yes, yes, friend Ossep, now show what you can do! I would burn ten candles to have you in my power.
[*Exit, right, taking the account book*].

Scene VI
Khali. Salome

KHALI [*entering from the left*]. Such a bold creature I never saw before in my life! [*Calling through the window*:] Come in! come in! I pray! Do you hear, Salome? I am calling you. Come in here a moment [*coming back from the window*]. She is coming. Wait, you insolent thing! I will give you a setting-out such as no one has ever given you before!

SALOME [*dressed in the latest fashion, with a parasol in her hand; enters at middle door*]. Why did you call me? Good-morning! How are you?
[*They shake hands*].

KHALI. Thank you. Pray sit down. [*They both sit down.*] So you have betrothed your daughter?

SALOME. Yes, dear Khali. God grant that we soon hear of

129

your Nino's like good-fortune! I betrothed her last evening. I found a good husband for her. He is as handsome as a god. I can scarcely stand for joy!

KHALI. Yes, make yourself important about it!

SALOME [*offended*]. What is this? What does it mean?

KHALI. You owed us a favor, and you have done it for us.

SALOME. What have I done to you?

KHALI. You could not do more, indeed. You have cheated me out of a son-in-law. Is not that enough?

SALOME. But, my dear Khali, what kind of things are you saying to me? What do you mean by it?

KHALI. Be still! be still! I know well enough how it was.

SALOME. May I go blind if I know what you are talking about!

KHALI. Didn't you know very well that I wished to give my daughter to him?

SALOME. I don't understand you! You said no earthly word to me about it.

KHALI. Even if I have not said anything about it, someone has certainly told you of it.

SALOME. No one has said a word about it.

KHALI. She lies about it, beside! Isn't that shameful?

SALOME. Satan lies. What are you accusing me of?

KHALI. And you really did not know that I wished to give him my daughter?

130

SALOME. And if I had known it? When a man wants to marry, they always speak of ten, and yet he marries only one.

KHALI. So you knew it very well? Why did you lie, then?

SALOME. You are out of your head! How was I to find it out? Did you send word by anyone that you were going to give your daughter to the man? In what way am I to blame for it? You knew as much as I did. You treated with him just as I did and sent marriage brokers to him.

KHALI. I approached him first.

SALOME. O my dear, the flowers in the meadow belong not to those who see them first, but to those who pluck them.

KHALI. You did not wait. Perhaps I would have plucked them.

SALOME. And why didn't you pluck them?

KHALI. You wouldn't let me. Do you think I do not know that you promised him more than we did?

SALOME. May I go blind! Khali, how can you say that? How much did you promise him?

KHALI. How much did we promise him? Ha! ha! as though you did not know it! Eight thousand rubles.

SALOME. Then you promised more than we did, for we can give him only 7,000.

KHALI. You surely do not think me so stupid as to believe that!

SALOME. As sure as I wish my Nato all good fortune, what I say is true.

KHALI. And you think that I believe you?

SALOME. What? What do you say? Would I swear falsely about my daughter?

KHALI. Of course it is so! Would he let my 8,000 go to take your 7,000?

SALOME. I am not to blame for that. Probably your daughter did not please him, since he did not want her.

KHALI. What fault have you to find with my daughter? As though yours were prettier, you insolent woman, you!

SALOME [standing up]. You are insolent! Is it for this you called me in? Can your daughter be compared to my Nato? Is it my fault that your daughter has a wide mouth?

KHALI. You have a wide mouth yourself; and your forward daughter is not a bit prettier than mine!

SALOME. What! you say she is forward? Everyone knows her as a modest and well-behaved girl, while everybody calls yours stupid. Yes, that is true; and if you want to know the truth, I can tell it to you—it is just on that account that he would not have her.

KHALI. Oh, you witch, you! You have caught the poor young man in your nets and deceived him. I would like to know where you are going to get the 7,000 rubles.

SALOME. That is our affair. I would rather have broken my leg than to have come in here.

KHALI. He is up to the ears in debt and is going to give such a dowry!

SALOME [coming back]. Even if we are in debt, we have robbed nobody,
as you have.

KHALI [springing up]. 'Tis you who steal; you! You are a

thief! Look out for yourself that I do not tear the veil off your head, you wicked witch, you!

SALOME [*holding her veil toward her*]. Try it once. I would like to see how you begin it. You have altogether too long a tongue, and are only the daughter-in-law of the cobbler Matus.

KHALI. And what better are you? You are a gardener's daughter, you insolent thing!

SALOME. You are insolent, yourself! Do not think so much of yourself—everyone knows that you have robbed the whole world, and only in that way have gotten up in the world.

KHALI. Oh, you good-for-nothing!
[*Throws herself on Salome and tears her veil off*].

SALOME. Oh! oh!
[*Gets hold of Khali's hair*].

KHALI. Oh! oh!

SALOME. I'll pull all your hair out!
[*Astonished, she holds a lock in her hand*].

Enter Ossep.

OSSEP. What do I see?

KHALI [*tearing the lock from Salome's hand*]. May I be blind!
[*Exit embarrassed*].

SALOME [*arranging her veil*]. Oh, you monkey, you!

OSSEP. What is the meaning of this?

SALOME. God only knows how it came to this. I was walking quietly in the street and she called me in and tore the veil from my head because I, as she said, took her daughter's suitor away from her.

OSSEP. It serves you right! That comes from your having secrets from me and promising him 7,000 rubles instead of 6,000.

SALOME. I would rather have broken a leg than come into this horrid house. I did it only out of politeness. I wish these people might lose everything they have got [*pinning her veil*]. At any rate, I punished her for it by pulling off her false hair. If she tells on herself now, she may also tell about me. She got out of the room quickly, so that no one would find out that her hair was as false as everything else.

OSSEP. It would be best for us if the earth opened and swallowed us up.

SALOME [*crying*]. Am I, then, so much to blame here?

OSSEP. Really, you look splendid! Go! go! that no one sees you here. It is not the first time that you have put me in a dilemma. Go! and pray God to change noon into midnight and make the streets dark, so that no one sees that you have a torn veil on your head.

SALOME [*wiping away her tears*]. God only knows everything I have to suffer from you!

OSSEP [*alone*]. Great heaven! how this world is arranged! When one trouble comes to a man a second comes along, too, and waits at his door. When I am just about ready to cope with the first, in comes the second and caps the climax. I don't know which way to turn with all my debts; and now this women's quarrel will be laid at my door.

Scene VII

BARSSEGH [*coming in, angry*]. I will show him that I am a man!

134

OSSEP. Good-morning!

BARSSEGH. I want neither "good-morning" nor any other wish from you. You have, I suppose, come to help your wife. Give me a blow, too, so the measure will be full. This is surely the interest on the money you owe me.

OSSEP. Calm yourself. What, indeed, do you want?

BARSSEGH. Do you, then, believe that I will overlook my wife's hair being pulled out? That I will not pardon.

OSSEP. What is there to pardon? Your wife tore my wife's veil from her head.

BARSSEGH. A veil is not hair.

OSSEP. For heaven's sake, stop! Is a women's spat our affair?

BARSSEGH. Say what you wish, but I will do what pleases me.

OSSEP. Calm yourself; calm yourself.

BARSSEGH. Yes, yes; I will calm you, too.

OSSEP. Believe me; it is unworthy of you.

BARSSEGH. She has torn her veil, he says. What is a veil, then? A thing that one can buy, and at most costs two rubles.

OSSEP. The hair was also not her own. Why do you worry yourself about it? For a two-ruble veil she tore a two-kopeck band. The band is there, and she can fasten the hair on again.

BARSSEGH. No, you can't get out of it that way. I will not pardon her for this insolence.

OSSEP [aside]. Great heaven!

135

BARSSEGH. You'll see! you'll see!

OSSEP. Do what you will! I did not come to you on that account. You sent for me by Micho?

BARSSEGH. Yes, you are right. Have you brought me my money? Give it to me, quick!

OSSEP. How you speak to me! Am I your servant, that you speak so roughly? You surely do not know whom you have before you. Look out, for if I go for you, you will sing another tune.

BARSSEGH. That has not happened to me yet! He owes me money, and even here he makes himself important!

OSSEP. Do you think because I owe you money I shall stand your insults? I speak politely to you, and I demand the same from you.

BARSSEGH. Enough of that! Tell me whether you have brought the money or not.

OSSEP. Have I ever kept back from you any of your money? Why should I do it to-day?

BARSSEGH. Then give it to me now.

OSSEP. You said at that time—

BARSSEGH. I know nothing of that time.

OSSEP. What is the matter with you? You speak as if in a dream.

BARSSEGH. Whether I speak as in a dream or not, give me the money, and have done with it.

OSSEP [*takes a chair and sits down*]. You are mistaken, my dear Mr. Barssegh; you are mistaken. Sit down, pray.

BARSSEGH [*ironically*]. Thank you very much.

OSSEP. You will surely not take back your word?

BARSSEGH. Hand over the money.

OSSEP. What has happened to you? You speak like a madman.

BARSSEGH. It is all the same to me however I speak.

OSSEP. When I gave you the 5,000 rubles that time, did not you say that I was to pay the rest in a month?

BARSSEGH [*sitting down*]. And if I did say so, what does it amount to? I need it now.

OSSEP. You should have said so at the time and I would not have paid out my money in other ways. How comes it that you demand it so suddenly? I am no wizard, I am sure, to procure it from the stars for you.

BARSSEGH. You may get it wherever you want to. I need it, and that settles it.

OSSEP. Just heaven! Why did you give me a month's grace and reckon on an additional twelve per cent. for it?

HARSSEGH. What kind of grace? Have you anything to show for it?

OSSEP. Isn't your word enough? Why do we need a paper in addition?

BARSSEGH. I didn't give you my word.

OSSEP. What? You did not give it? You admitted it just a few minutes
ago.

BARSSEGH. No, I said nothing about it.

OSSEP [*standing*]. My God! what do I see and hear? You are a merchant and tread your word under foot. Shame on you! [*Takes him by the arm and leads him to the mirror.*] Look! look at your face! Why do you turn pale?

BARSSEGH. Let me go!

OSSEP [*holding him fast by the sleeve*]. How can you be so unscrupulous? Look! How pale your lips are!

BARSSEGH. Let me go! [*Freeing himself.*] You act exactly as though you were the creditor.

OSSEP. No, you are the creditor. I would rather be swallowed up alive by the earth than be such a creditor as you are. What do you think you will be in my eyes after this?

BARSSEGH. I tell you, hand out my money or I will lay your note before the court immediately! I would only like to know where you are going to get the dowry for your daughter. You will pay over my money to your son-in-law, will you, and give me the go-by?

OSSEP. Give yourself no trouble! Even if you should beg me now, I would not keep your money. To-morrow at this time you shall have it, and then may the faces turn black of those who still look at you.

BARSSEGH. I want it at once.

OSSEP. Then come with me. You shall have it. The sooner a man is rid of a bad thing, the better it is. Give me the note! No, don't give it to me, for you don't trust me. You are not worthy of trusting me. Take it yourself and come with me. We will go at once to the bazaar, sell it, then you can have your money. I may lose something by it. It makes no difference. It is easier to bear this misfortune than to talk to you. Do you hear? Shall we go?

BARSSEGH. What do you mean?

OSSEP. Get the note, I tell you! Don't you hear?

BARSSEGH. What kind of a note?

OSSEP. Rostom's note.

BARSSEGH. Rostom's' note? What is this note to you?

OSSEP. What is it to me? It is no word, indeed, that you can deny. It is a document.

BARSSEGH. What is it to you that I have this document in my hands? That is mine and Rostom's business.

OSSEP. Yours and Rostom's business! [*Pauses.*] It is, I see, not yet enough that you lie. You are a thief and a robber beside. What people say of you is really true; namely, that you have robbed everybody, and by this means have acquired your wealth. Yes, it is true that you have ruined twenty-five families; that you have put out their candle and lighted yours by it. Now I see, for the first time, that everything that people say about you is true. Now I believe, indeed, that these chairs, this sofa, this mirror, your coat, your cane—in a word, every article that you call yours— represents some person you have robbed. Take my bones and add to them. Make the measure full. You have made your conscience a stone and will hear nothing; but I tell you, one day it will awake, and every object that lies or stands here will begin to speak and hold up to you your villanies. Then you can go and justify yourself before your Maker. Shame upon him who still calls you a human being!
[*Exit by the middle door*].

BARSSEGH. Ha! ha! ha!
[*Exit at the right*].

CURTAIN.

ACT THIRD
Scene I—Ossep's House

NATO [*stands before the mirror elegantly dressed, and, while she prinks, hums a European melody. Then she draws out of her pocket a little photograph and speaks to herself while looking in the mirror*]. O my treasure! my treasure! [*Presses the photo to her breast and kisses it.*] *Mon chèr!* Come; we will dance. [*Dances around the table.*] Tra-la-la, Tra-la-la. [*Sits down at the right.*] Alexander; my Alexander; dear Alexander! Yes, you are really an angel. Why are you so handsome? You have black eyes and I also have black. Then arched eyebrows just like me. [*Touches her eyebrows.*] A pretty little mustache, which I lack. Which of us is more beautiful, I or you? You are handsomest; no, I am handsomest [*springing up*]. We will see at once. [*Looks at herself in the mirror and then at the photograph. Enter Alexander at the middle door*].

NATO [*without noticing Alexander*]. No, you are the more beautiful!
[*Kisses the photograph*].
[*Alexander approaches softly and kisses Nato*].

NATO [*frightened*]. Oh!

ALEXANDER. No, you are the more beautiful, Natalie, dear. *Ma chère Nathalie!*

NATO. *O mon chèr Alexandre!* How you frightened me!

ALEXANDER [*putting his arm around her*]. Let me kiss you again, and your fright will pass away. [*Kisses her.*] Give me a kiss just once!

NATO [*kissing him*]. There, you have one.

ALEXANDER. Well, I ought to allow you to kiss me. Am I not worth more than that piece of paper?
[*Takes her by the hand; they sit down on sofa at the right.*

140

NATO. They have come to congratulate us.

ALEXANDER. Yes, your grandmother, your aunts, and your cousins. Nato, shall you give evening parties like this?

NATO [*smiling*]. Ha! ha! ha! No such *soirées* as this, my dear Alexander. Two evenings every month we will give little dances, either on Tuesdays or Thursdays. Which is better? Do you not think, Alexander, that Thursday will be best?

ALEXANDER [*with a grimace*]. As you wish, *chère Nathalie*. If you like, you can give a *soirée* every week.

NATO. No, twice a month is better. Sophie, who is now Madame Jarinskaja, gives only two *soirées* in a month.

ALEXANDER. Very well, Nato dear.

NATO. That is agreed, then. And every Thursday we will dance at the Casino. [*Alexander makes another grimace.*] Mind, now! every Thursday.

ALEXANDER. Do you like to visit the Casino?

NATO [*laying her hand on his shoulder*]. Who doesn't like to visit it? Is there another place where one can amuse one's self better? The beautiful long *salon*! the *boudoir*! the beautiful music and the rich costumes! How beautiful they all are! [*Embracing Alexander.*] We will dance together, and when we are tired, we will go into the mirror-room and rest ourselves and talk and laugh.

ALEXANDER. And then we will dance again and rest ourselves, and talk and laugh again.

NATO. It will be splendid! [*Kisses him.*] I will dress beautifully *à la mode*, so that everyone will say, "Look! look! what a charming woman Madame Marmarow is!" And then, dear Alexander, we will subscribe for a box at the theatre for Fridays.

ALEXANDER [*making another grimace aside*]. She's piling it on.

NATO. And do you know where? In the upper tier at the left, near the foyer.

ALEXANDER. Wouldn't it be better to subscribe for two evenings a week?

NATO. Wouldn't it cost too much?

ALEXANDER. What has that to do with it? Do you think I could deny you any pleasure? No! no! you shall have everything.

NATO [*embracing him*]. *Chèr Alexandre*! do you really love me so much?

ALEXANDER. I cannot tell you at all how much I love you. Right at our first meeting I fell in love with you!

NATO. I don't believe it! I don't believe it! All young men talk so!

ALEXANDER. Ha! ha! ha! Do you think I am like them? With them the tongues have nothing to do with the heart; but my tongue speaks what is here!
[*Strikes himself on the breast.*

NATO [*ironically*]. I know! I know! If I had no dowry you would not marry me.

ALEXANDER. Nato dear, you wrong me! *ma chère*! As if the dowry made any difference! *Fi donc*!

NATO. Then you really love me so much?

ALEXANDER. Very, very much, Nato dear. You can put me to the test if you will.

NATO. Do you know, my piano is not fit to use!

142

ALEXANDER [*smoothing his hair—aside*]. Something new again.

NATO. Buy me a new piano. To-day I saw one at a store; it cost 500 rubles.

ALEXANDER. Five hundred rubles! You cannot buy a decent piano for that!

NATO. Dear Alexander!

ALEXANDER. Be patient awhile, Nato dear. One of my friends brought a piano from abroad that cost 1,000; yes, even 1,500 rubles.

NATO. My sweetheart; my dear sweetheart! [*Kissing him.*] I will come right back. [*Rises.*] I must go and prepare for our reception or mamma will be angry. Tra-la-la.
[*Exit at left*].

ALEXANDER [*alone, springing up*]. Ha! ha! ha! *soirées*, balls at the club, box at the theatre, dresses and ornaments after the latest fashion! Am I a millionaire? I would have nothing against it if I had the money to do it. She acts as though she was going to bring 50,000 rubles dowry into the house. No, Natalie, that will all come later. In ten or twenty years, perhaps, I will set up a carriage; but it is not even to be thought of now. Indeed, I don't know, where it will lead to if she makes such demands on me every day. It will lead to quarrels and unpleasantness, and it will be all up with my economizing. No, indeed, Natalie, it will be no easy thing to satisfy you. Why did I not think of this sooner? Let her talk, and demand what she will. I will do what pleases me.

NATO [*enter right; speaks to someone behind the scenes*]. I will come at once. I am coming. Come, Alexander, let us go into the garden. Mamma must go upstairs, and the guests will be all alone in the garden.

ALEXANDER. I am waiting for your father, Nato dear, I have something important to discuss with him.

143

NATO. Why, we will soon return, and by that time father will be home. Do you want to sit here alone?

ALEXANDER. Well, we will go.

NATO. Come! come! I want to introduce you to my coquettish aunt.
[*Mimics her while making a courtesy, and makes faces. Alexander, shaking his head, goes out with Nato noisily through middle door.*

Scene II
Salome. Chacho.

CHACHO. No, indeed, Salome. She behaves too boldly. You must give her a warning. Such self-confidence I have I never before seen in a girl.

SALOME. That is all a matter of fashion! What is to be done? [*Shuffling the cards*].

CHACHO [*seating herself*]. When one thinks how the times have changed, one grows dizzy! When I was engaged, my love, I dared not open my mouth; it was as if they had put a lock on it. Indeed, I dared not look anyone in the face, even, and kept my eyes always cast down, as if glued fast to the floor.

SALOME. How could anyone endure all that? The eyes are made to look with, I hope, and the tongue to speak! I wouldn't have borne it. It is well that those times are past. I should die of such a life.

CHACHO. Oh, your present times are the true ones! Isn't this shameful, now, what goes on here? All the money that the husband can make in a week, the wife loses at play in a single evening. Is that widow, the stout one, going to play with you? She is surely more than fifty years old.

SALOME. Of course! we wouldn't play at all without her.

144

CHACHO. That is the best of all. Why, she has a married daughter as old as you are!

SALOME. What of that? Whoever has money can always play. But what do you say to the wife of blind Gigoli? She hasn't enough to eat, but gives herself airs before us just the same.

CHACHO. Don't talk to me about her! A few weeks ago she pawned a silver pitcher to one of our neighbors for five rubles without her husband's knowledge. God punished her for it, for that same evening she lost it all at cards. I should like to know how she is going to redeem the pitcher.

SALOME [*arranging her dress before the mirror*]. Yes, yes; no one can take her measure better than I.
[*Enter Ossep*].

OSSEP [*angrily*]. And what have you gotten ready for again?

SALOME. What was to be done? Look and see how many guests there are in the garden!

OSSEP. It was very wrong of them to come here. Has no one invited them, then? They should have asked me first.

SALOME. You are a singular being! We have betrothed our daughter and they were obliged to come and congratulate us.

OSSEP. Congratulate! As though my joy went to their hearts! On the contrary, they would enjoy it if I had a misfortune; they could put their heads together and criticize and laugh at me.

CHACHO. What are you so ill-humored about? For the last two days you have been intolerable.

OSSEP. If I could unbosom myself to you and show you my heart, you would comprehend what the cause of it is.

CHACHO. God protect you from all evil!

OSSEP. Am I not right? Tell me yourself! This is not the time for card-playing. Why have they come, then? If they wished to congratulate us, they could come separately. How does it happen that they all thought of us at once? Perhaps each has sent word to the other that Salome has betrothed her daughter and they have all taken advantage of the opportunity to come. Of course only for the sake of those damned cards! This one or that one has probably been invited by her [*pointing to Salome*]. She sent word to them, "Come to us, I pray! X and Z are already here." [*To Salome:*] Say, isn't that so?

SALOME. What nonsense he talks! Ought they not to know at your uncle's house that we have betrothed our daughter? I was obliged to give them some information about it, was I not?

OSSEP. And to whom beside?

SALOME. Whom else? Your cousins. And I have just sent for your sister-in-law.

OSSEP [*anxiously*]. For what purpose? She could have come another time just as well.

SALOME. How useless it is to talk so! You understand nothing at all about the matter. Your relatives would take offence in every possible way if I did not invite them. They would not speak to me for a year!

OSSEP. Great heaven! I wish they were struck blind! [*Sits down and pulls at the end of the table-cloth*]. I would take pleasure in throwing them all out!

SALOME. I have no time to dispute with you.
[*Exit at left, angry*].

OSSEP. Great heaven! have women been created only to bleed the men?

CHACHO. Don't excite yourself so, dear Ossep. What you

146

say is in every way pure facts. But you must overlook something now and then. It can't be helped now; they are all here; you cannot chase them out of the house. The whole city would be stirred up about it.

OSSEP. And what will people say when to-morrow or the day after my creditors come and chase me out of my house?

CHACHO. Oh, don't talk about such things!

OSSEP [*sitting down at the card-table*]. That's easily said. But let me tell you, I feel as though the house was going to fall down on top of me.

CHACHO. What has happened, Ossep?

OSSEP. They say Barssegh Leproink has brought action against me.

CHACHO. What? Brought action against you?

OSSEP. I owe him money, and on that account he holds the knife at my throat.

CHACHO. God bless me!

OSSEP. The wicked fellow has my note, and another security beside, and yet he will not wait.

CHACHO. His match for wickedness cannot be found in the whole world.

OSSEP. No, not another such miserable scoundrel! I expect every moment to be notified, and have no idea where I can get the money. Everyone I have asked to help me has refused me. I can borrow no more on my note, and I cannot sell my goods at half price. That everyone must understand. They all show their claws as soon as they find out the position I am in. Salome is to blame for all this; the 7,000 rubles she promised is the cause of it all. I would like to know who will pay them to him now.

CHACHO. You talk nonsense! You will make your daughter unhappy forever, Ossep.

OSSEP. I am still more unhappy myself. But let us see what the coming day brings forth. I still have hope of one. Perhaps he will supply me with money.

CHACHO. How could you trust the scamp so blindly? Is such want of thought consistent with reason?

OSSEP. What is the use of reason in this? I have always said I could not stand the expense that now everybody assumes. If a man conducts his business honestly, he makes little profit; and as for a dishonest business, I am not fit for that! So I have suffered one reverse after another; and where I was most vulnerable I have been hit at last.

CHACHO. Heavens! what do I hear? Why don't I sink into the earth?

OSSEP. In our line of trade only a few persons carry on their business with their own money. Most of us have to borrow. When I sell goods to one, I pay my debt to the other. I sell goods to the third and pay to the fourth; and so it goes in a circle, like a wheel drawing water, until one falls in the hands of a man who draws the needle out of the knitting and everything falls in pieces. Who is in a position to fight against such conditions? One must pay the store rent and the clerk's salary, and beside that the interest on the working capital. Then there are the goods that are spoiled or stolen— and here at home! [*Striking the cards.*] All this rubbish and more beside! [*Striking the table again.*] And the women are to blame for all this; if my wife had not promised 7,000 rubles, without my knowledge, the betrothal would not have taken place, and this bad luck would not have come to me. But where does one find among our women insight and forethought? For model women give me some foreign countries. There the women stand by the men in everything: the wife of a cook is a cook; the wife of a writer, a writer; the wife of a merchant is in every case a merchant. They earn jointly and spend jointly. With us the man is here only to make money for them, so that they [*striking the table*] may kill time with foolish things like this.

CHACHO. Say, rather, that times are changed; for the men also sit at the club all day and play cards.

OSSEP. Ho! ho! As though women did not play cards also! Formerly the cards were solely our diversion; but they have taken them away from us. Don't worry yourself; with God's help they will be learning to play billiards. Why do you dwell upon the fact that the men play cards? One in a thousand plays; while of a thousand women, nine hundred play. Men are always more moderate. They see that the times are hard, and have given up most of their earlier pleasures. Where are the banquets that used to be given, one after another? Where are the drinking-places where the music played? They have given them up; and the women are just like they were, only worse. To-day they arrange a picnic, to-morrow a little party, and so on. The men stand gaping at them, and the children are left to the servants. If I could take the law into my own hands, I'd soon set them right.
[*Paces to and fro in anger*].

CHACHO [*rising, aside*]. He is right. All that he says is pure truth.
[*Exit left*].

Scene III
Ossep. Then Alexander.

OSSEP. O dear! O dear!
[*Stands near fireplace; rests head on hand and remains motionless*].

ALEXANDER [*enter right*]. You have come, father?
[*Silence—comes near Ossep.*] Father.

OSSEP. Ah! Alexander [*offering his hand*]. Please sit down. Have you just come?

ALEXANDER. No; I have been here a long time. I was in the garden.

OSSEP. What is the news?
[*Both sit down*].

ALEXANDER. Nothing, except that I wish to have a wedding next week.

OSSEP. So soon?

ALEXANDER. Yes; my chief goes soon to Petersburg, and I want him to be at the wedding.

OSSEP. And can't we wait till he comes back?

ALEXANDER. That would be too long.

OSSEP. Very well. As you wish.

ALEXANDER [*stammering*]. But—my dear father—

OSSEP. I understand; I understand. You want me to pay over the money at once?

ALEXANDER. Yes, my dear father, if it is possible.

OSSEP. I am sorry to confess that at the present moment I have no money at hand. You must wait a little. If you wish to marry without money, that is your affair.

ALEXANDER. You amaze me!

OSSEP. It is better for me to tell you this than to deceive you. You know the law to some extent. Tell me, if I owe someone money on a note, can my creditor bring action against me and put an execution on me without having me called before the court?

ALEXANDER. Is the note attested by a notary?

OSSEP. Yes.

ALEXANDER. He has the right to come to your house and have everything put under seal.

OSSEP. Without first bringing me into court?

ALEXANDER. Yes, without court proceedings.

OSSEP. But if he has received on account of this debt the note of a third person?

ALEXANDER. That is another thing. Have you a receipt for it?

OSSEP. No; but I can take my oath on it.

ALEXANDER. According to law you must first pay the money and then produce proofs that you gave him the other document.

OSSEP [*excited*]. Is that true?

ALEXANDER. Yes, it is so.

OSSEP [*wringing his hands and springing up*]. Then I am ruined. [*A silence. Nato's voice is heard outside.*] Alexander, they are calling you.

ALEXANDER [*approaching Ossep*]. What is it? For God's sake tell me the truth.

OSSEP. There, there. Go out first. They are calling you.

ALEXANDER [*aside, taking his hat*]. So far as I see, I am ruined also.
[*Exit*].

OSSEP [*alone*]. What do I not suffer! If they really come here I shall perish through shame. Where can I find so much money in such a hurry? One must have time for it, and that fellow may come to-day even—perhaps this minute. Then I am lost—who will trust me then? My creditors will tie a rope around my neck and prevent me from saying a word in my own behalf. "Pay us," they will cry; "pay us!" O Salome, Salome!

Enter Gewo

OSSEP. There he is.

GEWO. Good-evening, Ossep.

OSSEP. You have come, too. You want your money, too? Yes, choke me; double my debt; say that I owe you, not 2,000 rubles, but 4,000. Speak! You are my creditor; speak! Have no pity on me. You want your money—why do you wait, then? Slay me; tear my heart out of my body; hack me in pieces and sell it piece by piece, so that your money shall not be lost. [*Gewo wipes his eyes.*] Weep, weep, for your money is lost. I am bankrupt—bankrupt!

GEWO [*embracing Ossep*]. Dear Ossep, dear Ossep!

OSSEP. You say "dear" to me? Yet you are my creditor.

GEWO. Take courage; be a man!

OSSEP. What kind of a man? I am a good-for-nothing; I have lost my good name [*weeping*]. My good name is gone. [*Wipes his eyes.*]

GEWO. God is merciful, dear Ossep.

OSSEP. God and heaven have taken their mercy from me. You see now where the marriage of my daughter has led me? If I could at least pay you everything I owe you—that I must do at any price.

GEWO. What are you saying, Ossep? If I had the means I would go on your bond. Why should I be your friend otherwise?

152

OSSEP. If you had money, dear Gewo, you would not be my friend, nor have such a good heart. Stay poor as you are, so that I shall not lose your friendship. Only your sympathy is left me in this world. I would not like to lose your friendship. In this one day I have suffered everything. No one has shown interest in me; no one has given proof of his sympathy— neither my uncle, nor my brother, nor my nephew. When they saw I was near my last breath, they all forsook me and shut the door in my face.

GEWO. Come with me; perhaps we will find help somewhere.

OSSEP. There can be no more talk of help.

GEWO. Come, come; there is still a way out.

OSSEP. What way out can there be?

GEWO. Come, come; let us not delay.

OSSEP. But tell me how is it to be managed?

GEWO. Come, come! I will tell you on the way.

OSSEP. What you say sounds very strange; tell me what it is. Speak, what has occurred? Don't fear! Don't spare me! Whatever happens cannot be worse than what has happened; they have already sent a bullet into my heart, and what worse can they do to me, except tear open my breast and take my heart out? Speak; what is it? Have they put seals on my store?

GEWO. Come and you will see.

OSSEP. They have put seals on it, then?

GEWO. I tell—

OSSEP. You are ruined, Ossep. [*Rushes to the table, seizes the box and scatters the cards; some fall on the floor.*] Now

you may play; now you may play.
[*Exit*].

GEWO. Too bad; too bad about him!
[*Follows him*].

Scene IV

*Enter Salome, Martha, Nino, Pepel, and many well-dressed
ladies, followed by two footmen carrying candelabra and
lamps, which they put on the table.*

SALOME. Take seats, please. The cards are already here.

MARTHA. How pretty it is, isn't it? The cards are already
dealt.
[*The ladies converse smilingly with one another*].

SALOME [*stepping forward and noticing the cards on the
floor*]. What is this? Who can have done it?

MARTHA. Probably the cats ran over the table.

SALOME. I cannot think how it could have happened!
Please sit down.

Enter Nato and her friends

SALOME [*collecting the cards*]. Who can have done it?
Nato, did you do it?

NATO. No, mamma, I did not touch them.

SALOME [*to the guests*]. Sit down, I beg.
[*All the guests sit down at the table, Nato and her friends sit
on the other side of the stage. Salome, standing, deals the
cards which the guests hand one to the other. Then they pay
in the stakes to Salome, which she lays on the table in front
of her*].

Enter Alexander

NATO [*going to meet Alexander*]. Alexander, why were you so long?

ALEXANDER. I was obliged to be [*leading Nato aside excitedly, and in a whisper:*] I have something to say to you.

NATO [*in a whisper*]. What makes your hand tremble?

ALEXANDER. They have brought action against your father in the courts.

NATO. What! For what reason?

ALEXANDER. Because of debts.

NATO. Who told you so?

ALEXANDER. Your father himself.

NATO [*laughing aloud*]. Ha! ha! ha! [*Whispering:*] My father has no debts.

ALEXANDER. Well, he told me so himself.

NATO. He was joking. Don't believe him.
[*Goes over to her friends, laughing*].

ALEXANDER. Well, I can't make it out. I am not so stupid, however. Until I have the money in my hands I will not cross this threshold again.

SALOME. Let us begin.
[*Guests begin to play*].

Scene V

Enter Chacho

CHACHO [*coming from left*]. Get this stuff out of the way.

SALOME. What is the matter? What has happened?

CHACHO. What was to happen? We are ruined. [*Behind the scenes are heard threatening voices:*] "Here! Yes! No." [*Then Ossep's voice:*] "Come in, come in."

CHACHO [*to Salome*]. Do you not hear them?

Enter Barssegh through middle door

BARSSEGH. This is really splendid! I work for my daily bread, and you illuminate your house on my money.

CHACHO [*to Salome*]. Now you have it.

SALOME [*rising*]. Are you mad? Show him out.

BARSSEGH. I will show you pretty soon who is to be shown out.

SALOME. Alexander, show this man out.

ALEXANDER [*to Barssegh*]. What do you want, sir? How can you indulge in such insolence?

BARSSEGH. That is not your affair, sir! I demand my money. Demand yours also if you can. You will be obliged to wait a long while for it.

CHACHO [*to Barssegh*]. Have you no conscience?

BARSSEGH. I want my money, and nothing more.
Enter Ossep, Gewo, a sheriff and his secretary, Dartscho, and several others.
OSSEP [*opening the door with both hands as he enters*].

156

Come in! come in! [*The others follow him.*] Play, play and laugh as much as you will over my misfortunes!

CHACHO [*aside*]. Now it is all over with us!

SALOME. Tell me, for God's sake, the meaning of this.

OSSEP. God will judge you and me also. [*To sheriff and others:*] Come, make your inventory, put your seals on everything—the house, the furniture, and on the cards, too.

BARSSEGH. Make an inventory of everything.
[*The sheriff lists furniture in the background and puts a ticket on each piece. The guests assemble, frightened, on the left side of the table*].

SALOME [*beating her head*]. Good heavens!

MARTHA. This is a disgrace for us as well.

CHACHO [*in a low voice to Martha*]. You at least should be silent.

OSSEP [*pointing to Barssegh*]. He has stripped me of my honor. Now you will honor and esteem him. He will arrange for your parties. Yes, he, the man who takes the shirt from my back and possesses himself of all my property.

ALEXANDER [*aside*]. I have my sister to thank for all this, who dragged me into this house.

OSSEP [*ironically*]. Alexander, look for a dowry elsewhere, for I can no longer give my daughter one.

ALEXANDER [*angry*]. What, you deride me as well! I don't belong to your class, sir!

OSSEP. And has it come to this!

ALEXANDER [*taking his hat*]. I have not acquired my present dignity to lose it through you.

OSSEP. Ha! ha! ha! His dignity!

ALEXANDER [*coming near Nato*]. I have loved you truly, Miss Nato, but I must give you up. I am not to blame for it. Farewell.
[*Goes to the door*].
[*Barssegh laughs for joy*].

OSSEP [*approaching Salome, who stands dismayed, takes her by the arm and points to the departing Alexander*]. There goes your official!

NATO [*standing at the left near the sofa*]. Alexander! Alexander! [*Exit Alexander.*] Dear Alexander.
[*Sitting down on the sofa, begins to cry*].

SALOME [*in a low tone, striking her brow with both hands*]. Why doesn't the earth open and swallow me?

OSSEP [*to Salome*]. Now you are punished, are you not? [*Turning to Barssegh:*] Take it all, now! Satisfy yourself! [*Takes off his coat.*] Take this also! [*Throws it to Barssegh.*] Yes, take it! [*Takes his cap from the table and throws it to Barssegh.*] Make off with this also; I need it no longer. [*Runs to and fro as if distracted*].

BARSSEGH [*in a low voice*]. Keep on giving!
[*Turns to sheriff and speaks softly to him*].

OSSEP [*taking up different articles from card table and throwing them on the floor*]. Take these also! Take these also! [*Taking a lighted candelabra and smashing it on the floor*] Stick that also down your throat!

SEVERAL OF THE GUESTS. The poor fellow is losing his wits.
[*Nato crying; her friends comfort her. Salome faints*].

CHACHO. Ossep! My dear Ossep!

GEWO [*embracing Ossep*]. Be calm, dear Ossep. You behave like a madman.

OSSEP [*after a pause*]. Gewo, I was mad when I settled in this city. This life is too much for me; it was not for me. I am ruined. I am a beggar. He is to be praised who comes off better than I.
[*Exit*].

SALOME [*with her hand on her brow sinks down on the sofa, groaning loudly*]. Ah!

GEWO. Poor Ossep!

BARSSEGH [*turns from Dartscho, to whom he has been speaking, to the sheriff*]. What are you gazing around for, sir? Keep on with your writing.
[*Sheriff looks at Barssegh in disgust, sits down by card table and writes*].

MARTHA [*to the guests*]. We have nothing more to look for here. [*Aside:*] A charming set!
[*Goes toward middle door; some ladies follow; others stand offended*].

CHACHO [*raising her eyes*]. Would that I had died long ago, so that I had not lived to see this unfortunate day!

CURTAIN.

Made in the USA
San Bernardino, CA
03 December 2015